Artificial Intelligence

T. D. Malhotra

M.Com., M.Sc., B.Ed., MCA (CS)

Retd Information Technology Senior Manager
from a Public Sector Organisation

8

- **Published by :**

  Nageen Prakashan Pvt. Ltd.

- **Registered Office :**

  Nageen Prakashan Pvt. Ltd.
  310, Western Kutchery Road,
  Meerut-250 002, U. P. (INDIA)
  Ph. : +91-121-2792600

- **Corporate Office :**

  Nageen Prakashan Pvt. Ltd.
  Vill. Salarpur, P.O. Rajpura
  Mawana Road,
  Meerut-250 001, U.P. (INDIA)
  Ph. : +91-121-2793401

  E-mail : info@nageenprakashan.com
  nageenprakashan@yahoo.com
  Visit us : www.nageenprakashan.in

- Latest Edition

- **ISBN :** 978-81-19514-25-0

- This edition can be exported from India only by the publisher.

- **Price :** ₹ **520.00** (In India)
  $ **27.00** (Outside India)

- **Printed at :**

  Nageen Print-Pack Pvt. Ltd.
  Vill. Salarpur, P.O. Rajpura
  Mawana Road,
  Meerut- 250 001, U.P. (INDIA)
  info@nageenprintpack.com

PREFACE

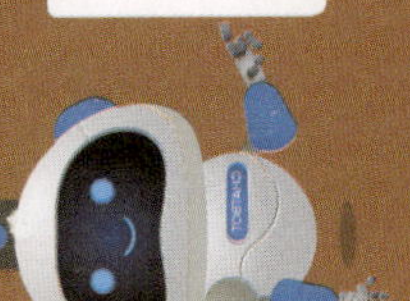

Keeping in view the need and importance of Artificial Intelligence (AI) in daily activities and for skill development, the subject of Artificial Intelligence has been introduced as a Skill Subject by the CBSE with the syllabus framework right from class 6 to senior secondary classes. For class 8, the subject of AI has been introduced to develop a readiness for understanding and appreciating Artificial Intelligence and its application in our lives. It focuses on helping learners understand the world of Artificial Intelligence and its applications through games, activities and multi-sensorial learning to become AI-ready. Moreover, it introduces the learners to three domains of AI and allows them to construct meaning of AI through interactive participation and engaging hands-on activities.

This book, on ***Artificial Intelligence*** for class 8, covers the extracts of all the ***modules: Excite, Relate, Purpose, Possibilities*** and ***AI Ethics*** in an age-appropriate manner. These topics have been covered with offline and online activities and projects.

In addition to the coverage of AI modules, **Introduction to Artificial Intelligence: Excite Module, Relate, Purpose, Possibilities, AI Ethics** and **Loops in Python** have also been explained at length. Besides, **Project Work: Artificial Intelligence-Based Home Automation, Scientists and Their Inventions in the Field of Artificial Intelligence, Fact File: Turing Test, Virtual Digital Assistants, Immersive Technologies, Quiz Time** and **Answer Sheet** for all chapters have also been added to enhance the learners' knowledge, understanding and application of AI.

I am thankful to **Shri Mohit Jain**, Managing Director, Nageen Prakashan, for taking great pains in bringing out the book in a multicoloured and attractive getup in a very short span of time. I am no less thankful to DTP Department and the diligent team for giving their best to shape up the book.

We welcome the suggestions for further improvement of the book. All suggestions will be acknowledged and taken care of in the next edition.

–Author

AGE-APPROPRIATE CONTENTS FOR ARTIFICIAL INTELLIGENCE MODULE

CLASS - 8

SUB-UNIT	LEARNING OUTCOMES	SESSION / ACTIVITY / PRACTICAL
1. EXCITE	• To identify and appreciate Artificial Intelligence and describe its applications in daily life.	Session: Introduction to AI and setting up the context of the curriculum
		Ice Breaker Activity: Dream Smart Home idea Learners to design a rough layout of floor plan of their dream smart home.
	• To relate, apply and reflect on the Human-Machine Interactions. • To identify and interact with the three domains of AI: Data, Computer Vision and Natural Language Processing.	Recommended Activity: The AI Game Learners to participate in games based on different AI domains. • Game 1: Rock, Paper and Scissors (based on data) • Game 2: Mystery Animal (based on Natural Language Processing - NLP) • Game 3: Emoji Scavenger Hunt (based on Computer Vision - CV)
	• To undergo an assessment for analysing progress towards acquired AI-Readiness skills.	Recommended Activity: AI Quiz (Paper Pen/Online Quiz)
	• To imagine, examine and reflect on the skills required for futuristic job opportunities.	Recommended Activity: Writing a Letter to one's future self Learners to write a letter to self-keeping the future in context. They will describe what they have learnt so far or what they would like to learn someday
2. RELATE	• Learners to relate to application of Artificial Intelligence in their daily lives.	Video Session: To watch a video Introducing the concept of Smart Cities, Smart Schools and Smart Homes
	• To unleash their imagination towards smart homes and build an interactive story around it. • To relate, apply and reflect on the Human–Machine interactions.	Recommended Activity: Write an Interactive Story Learners to draw a floor plan of a Home/ School/ City and write an interactive story around it using the Story Speaker extension in Google docs.
3. PURPOSE	• To understand the impact of Artificial Intelligence on Sustainable Development Goals to develop responsible citizenship.	Session: Introduction to UN Sustainable Development Goals
		Recommended Activity: Go Goals Board Game Learners to answer questions on Sustainable Development Goals
4. POSSIBILITIES	• To research and develop awareness of skills required for jobs of the future. • To imagine, examine and reflect on the skills required for the futuristic opportunities. • To develop effective communication and collaborative work skills.	Session: Theme-based research and Case Studies Learners will listen to various case-studies of inspiring start-ups, companies or communities where AI has been involved in real-life. Learners will be allotted a theme around which they need to search for present AI trends and have to visualise the future of AI in and around their respective theme.
		Recommended Activity: Job Ad Creating activity Learners to create a job advertisement for a firm describing the nature of job available and the skill-set required for it 10 years down the line. They need to figure out how AI is going to transform the nature of jobs and create the Ad accordingly.
5. AI ETHICS	• To understand and reflect on the ethical issues around AI.	Video Session: Discussing about AI Ethics Recommended Activity: Ethics Awareness Students play the role of major stakeholders and they have to decide what is ethical and what is not for a given scenario.
	• To gain awareness around AI bias and AI access.	Session: AI Bias and AI Access Discussing about the possible bias in data collection Discussing about the implications of AI technology
	• To let the students analyse the advantages and disadvantages of Artificial Intelligence.	Recommended Activity: Balloon Debate Students divide in teams of 3 and 2 teams are given the same theme. One team goes in affirmation to AI for their section while the other one goes against it. They have to come up with their points as to why AI is beneficial/ harmful for the society.

Additional Contents

- *Python Language*

INTRODUCTION

Computers create curiosity in the young brains. You may have questions but may not be able to find their answers because your teacher has given you the assignment. Your parents are busy and you cannot reach your classmate on the phone. Where can you go for help?

What Questions Does This Book Answer?

In this book, you will find a wealth of information, including the answers to 20 of the most commonly asked questions for your homework.

1. On the basis of capabilities, what are the different types of AI? (You can know about it on page 9.)
2. What are the different types of data required for artificial intelligence? (You will find the answer on page 17.)
3. What are the applications of natural language processing? (You can learn it on page 23.)
4. Do you want to relax and play a game in a group of two students? (Attempt the 'Game of Chance' by learning on page 28.)
5. What is deep text? (Look for the answer on page 44.)
6. What are the different types of smart home devices? (You will get your answer on page 49.)
7. What are the features of a smart city? (You will find the answer on page 55.)
8. What is human-machine interaction? (You can learn it on page 57.)
9. Which are the major components of sustainable development? (You can gain knowledge about them on page 68.)
10. How artificial intelligence can be important in assessing the life under water? (You will learn it on page 74.)
11. What is the role of virtual digital assistants? (You will find the answer on page 94.)
12. What is Blue Sky Analytics? (You can learn about it on page 100.)
13. How do AI biases take place? (See page 115.)
14. What are the privacy concerns in using artificial intelligence? (Gain knowledge on page 118.)
15. What are the different types of iterative statements in Python? (You can find answer on page 132.)
16. What is the role of Jump statements in loops? (Read about them on page 140.)
17. Write about any five scientists and their inventions in the field of artificial intelligence. (See page 160.)
18. Do you want to know about Turing Test? (You can learn about them on page 161.)
19. What are different types of immersive technologies? (You can gain knowledge about them on page 163.)
20. Do you want to check your skills in artificial intelligence? (Test yourself on page 164.)

CONTENTS

1

INTRODUCTION TO ARTIFICIAL INTELLIGENCE: EXCITE MODULE

Introduction

AI is a form of intelligence; a type of technology and a field of study. AI theory and development of computer systems (both machines and software) are able to perform tasks that normally require human intelligence. Artificial Intelligence covers a broad range of domains and applications and is expected to impact every field in the future. Overall, its core idea is building machines and algorithms which are capable of performing computational tasks that would otherwise require human like brain functions.

Let us study about Artificial Intelligence in details.

Learning Outcomes

Learners will be able to:

- Identify and appreciate Artificial Intelligence and describe its applications in daily life.

Coverage:

Introduction to AI and setting up the context of the curriculum.

To let the students, analyse the advantages and disadvantages of Artificial Intelligence.

ARTIFICIAL INTELLIGENCE

Computers are programmable devices. This makes it possible for users to make demands on these machines.

This means two things:

- The computer machine is capable of responding to intuitive demands.
- The user communicates in a language that a computer can understand (interpret).

Artificial Intelligence is the study of how to make the computers do things that at the moment, people do better.

John McCarthy (1927–2011) was a pioneer in the field of AI. He is known as the father of Artificial Intelligence. He also invented the term Artificial Intelligence.

Goals of AI

- To Create Expert Systems – Expert systems are those which show intelligent behaviour learn, demonstrate, explain and advice its users.

- To Implement Human Intelligence in Machines – AI aims at creating systems that can:
    - understand
    - think
    - learn
    - behave like humans.

What Contributes to AI?

Artificial intelligence is a science and technology that is based on various disciplines such as Computer Science, Biology, Psychology, Linguistic, Mathematics, Engineering. A major focus of AI is in the development of computer functions associated with human intelligence.

These functions are reasoning, learning and problem solving and AI aims at solving them with great accuracy and ease.

Types of AI Software

There are four different types of AI software in AI world:

- **Artificial Intelligence Platforms:** This will provide the platform for developing an application from start. Many built-in algorithms are provided in this approach.
- **Chatbots:** This software will give the effect that a human or person is doing a conversation.
- **Machine Learning Software:** Machine learning is the technique which makes the computer to learn through data.
- **Deep Learning Software:** It includes speech recognition, image recognition, etc.

> **Note**
> Computer Languages used for AI development are: LISP, PROLOG, Python. Out of these languages, Python is the modern language which is being extensively used in AI application development.

Top features of AI software include:

- Machine Learning
- Speech and Voice Recognition
- Virtual Assistant, etc.

AI combined with Machine learning is used to provide required functionality to the users. AI makes the business process a much simpler one.

AI software is used to build and develop an intelligent application from very beginning with the help of Machine Learning and Deep Learning.

AI Tools (Free Software)	Functionality
Azure Machine Learning Studio	Machine Learning
TensorFlow	Machine Learning
H2O AI	Machine Learning
Cortana	Virtual Assistant
IBM Watson	Question-answering system.
Amazon Alexa	Virtual Assistant
Google Assistant	Virtual Assistant

In addition to the software tools, programming languages best suited for AI are as follows (in the order of priority):

- Python
- Java
- R
- Julia
- Haskell
- Lisp
- C++
- PROLOG

What does Artificial Intelligence (AI) Mean?

Artificial Intelligence (AI) is a branch of Computer Science that emphasizes the creation of intelligent machines that work and react like humans.

Some of the activities, computers with artificial intelligence, include:

- Speech recognition
- Learning
- Planning
- Problem solving

TYPES OF ARTIFICIAL INTELLIGENCE

On the basis of capabilities, AI is of three types:

- Artificial Narrow Intelligence (ANI)
- Artificial General Intelligence (AGI)
- Artificial Super Intelligence (ASI)

Let us study these three types of AIs.

Artificial Narrow Intelligence

Narrow AI also called Weak AI, can perform a dedicated task with intelligence. This is the most common and currently available AI in the world of Artificial Intelligence.

Field of narrow AI is limited, as it is only trained for one specific task. Narrow AI cannot perform beyond its field. Therefore, it is also termed as weak AI. Narrow AI can fail in unpredictable ways if it goes beyond its limits.

Features of Narrow AI

- Narrow AI is goal-oriented.
- It is designed to perform singular tasks.
- It is very intelligent at completing the specific task.
- Narrow AI does not mimic or replicate human intelligence.
- Narrow AI's machine intelligence comes from the use of natural language processing (NLP) to perform tasks.

Facial recognition, speech recognition/voice assistants, driving a car or searching the Internet use the narrow AI.

Examples of Narrow AI

- Siri by Apple
- Alexa by Amazon
- Cortana by Microsoft
- IBM's Watson
- Image/facial recognition software
- Drone robots
- Email spam filters
- Social media monitoring tools
- Marketing content recommendations based on purchase behaviour
- Self-driving cars

Artificial General Intelligence (AGI)

General AI (AGI) is a strong Artificial Intelligence. It is a concept of machine that can perform any intellectual task with the efficiency of human. The idea behind the general AI is to make such an intelligent system which could be smarter and think like a human by its own.

Presently, there is no such system exist which could come under general AI and can perform any task as perfect as a human.

Systems with general AI are still under research and it will take a lot of efforts and time to develop such systems.

Artificial Super Intelligence (ASI)

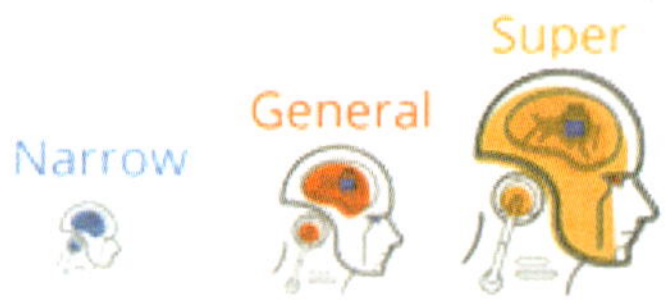

Super AI is a level of Intelligence of systems at which machines can surpass human intelligence, and can perform any task better than human. It is an outcome of general AI. Some key features of Super AI include the ability:

- to think
- to reason
- solve the puzzle
- make judgments and plans
- to learn and communicate by its own.

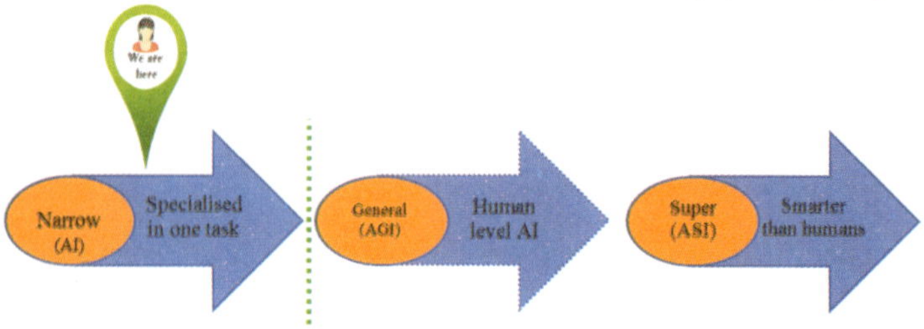

Super AI is still a hypothetical concept of Artificial Intelligence. Development of such systems in real is still a changing task.

Difference between Human and Machine Intelligence

- Human interpret by patterns whereas the machines interpret by set of rules and data.
- Human store and recall information by patterns whereas machines do it by searching algorithms.

  For Example:

  The number 8080808080 is easy to remember, store and recall for human as its pattern is simple.
- Humans can figure out the complete object even if some part of it is missing or distorted; whereas the machines cannot do this accurately.

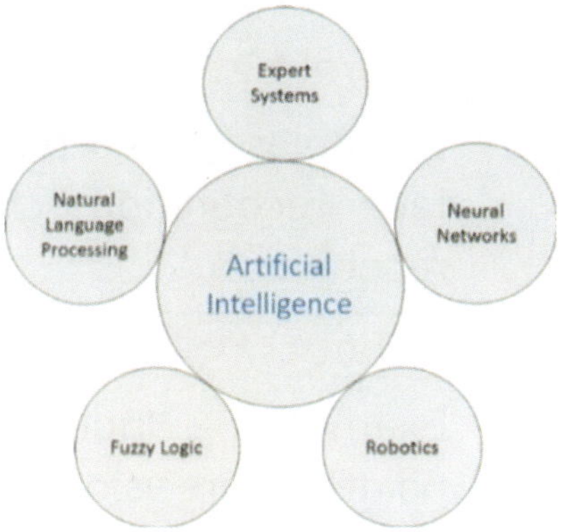

RESEARCH AREAS IN ARTIFICIAL INTELLIGENCE

The domain of artificial intelligence is huge. While proceeding, we consider the broadly common research areas in the domain of AI:

Speech and Voice Recognition

Both these terms are common in robotics, expert systems and natural language processing. Though these terms are used interchangeably, their objectives are different.

Working of Speech and Voice Recognition Systems

The spoken input of a user on a microphone, goes to sound card of the system. The converter converts the analog signal into equivalent digital signal for speech processing. The database is used to compare the sound patterns to recognize the spoken words. Finally, reverse feedback is given to the database.

This source-language text becomes input to the Translation Engine (TE). This TE converts it to the target language text. These systems are supported with interactive GUI, large database of vocabulary, etc.

Real-Life Applications of Research Areas

There are number of applications where AI is serving common people in their day-to-day lives. Let us have a look on these applications in the following table:

Sr. No	Research Areas	Real-Life Application
1	**Expert Systems** Examples - Flight-tracking systems, Clinical systems.	

2	**Natural Language Processing** Examples - Google Now feature, speech recognition, Automatic voice output.	
3	**Neural Networks** Examples – Pattern recognition systems such as face recognition, character recognition, handwriting recognition.	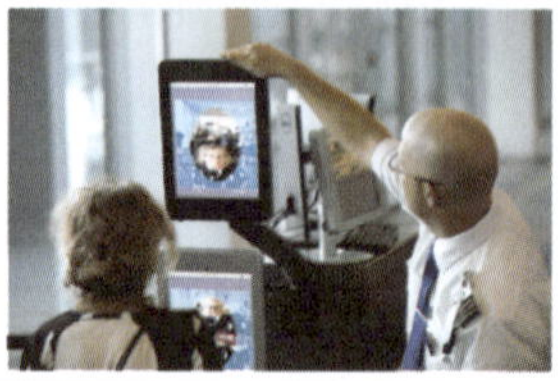
4	**Robotics** Examples – Industrial robots for moving, spraying, painting, precision checking, drilling, cleaning, coating, carving, etc.	
5	**Fuzzy Logic Systems** Examples – Consumer electronics, automobiles, etc.	

IMPORTANCE OF ARTIFICIAL INTELLIGENCE

Artificial Intelligence has become an important part of our daily life. Our life has been changed by AI because this technology is used in a number of day-to-day applications.

Using the intelligent machine speeds up your process of doing work and give you accurate results.

The introduction of AI brings the idea of error-free accurate world. This technology will slowly introduce in all the sectors to reduce human efforts and give accurate and faster result.

Role of AI in Bank and Financial System

Banks are using AI technology to handle different types of activities in their day-to-day business.

Using AI to handle activities like:

- financial operations
- lending decisions
- investing decisions in stock market, etc.
- Trading activities

Using AI in the Banking System helps the bank to handle their customers and give them a quick solution.

Role of AI in Medical Science

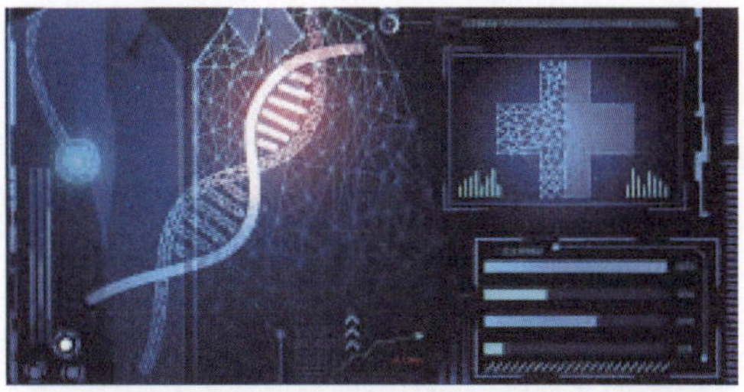

There are a number of applications in which AI are used and give reliable results in medical science. AI is used to create virtual personal health care assistants. These assistants are used for research and analytics.

Role of AI in Heavy Industries

In most of the big manufacturing companies, AI is mostly used in the production units. It is used in robots who give a different shape to an object and displace object from one place to another.

Role of AI in Air Transport

Air transport is one of the most systematic transports. Without AI, air transport cannot survive. A machine which is used in the planes for performing different functions is run on the basis of AI. Almost all the activities which are performed to control air transportation are based on AI technologies.

Role of AI in Gaming Zone

Computer and TV games got more development and updates in their fields with the change in technology. Once upon a time, a game "Super Mario" was considered as the best game. But now-a-days there are different gaming bots are introduced and you do not have to wait for other to play with yours. Bots are developed who will play with you.

APPLICATIONS OF AI IN DAILY LIFE

AI is important because it can help solve difficult issues in various industries, such as entertainment, education, health, commerce, transport and utilities. AI applications can be grouped into the following five categories:

- **Reasoning:** This is the ability to solve problems through logical deduction.

  For Example:

  Financial Management, legal assessment, loan application processing, games, etc.

- **Knowledge:** This is the ability to present knowledge about the world.

  For Example:

  Fraud prevention, drug creation, medical diagnosis, media recommendation.
- **Planning:** This is the ability to set and achieve goals.

  For Example:

  Inventory management, demand forecasting, predictive maintenance, physical and digital network optimization, navigation, scheduling, logistics.
- **Communication:** This is the ability to understand spoken and written language.

  For Example:

  Real-time translation of spoken and written languages, real-time transcription, intelligent assistants, voice control.
- **Perception:** Perception is the ability to infer things about the world via sounds, images and other sensory inputs.

  For Example:

  Medical diagnosis, autonomous vehicles, surveillance.

Examples of Artificial Intelligence

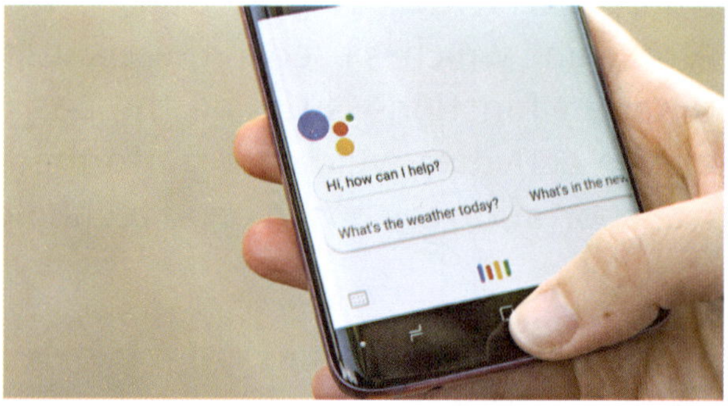

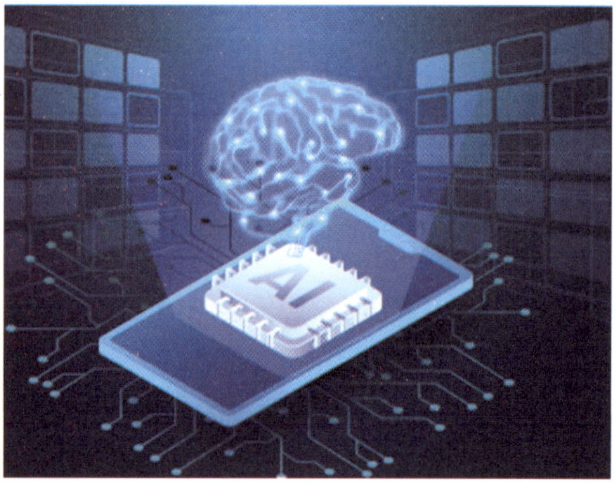

- **Smart Phone:** It has become the most indispensable product that we own today and we use it almost all the time. If you are using a smartphone, you are interacting with AI whether you are aware of it or not.

  There are some AI elements around us which most of us have some knowledge about.

  For Example:

  When you are using a smart assistant, whether it is Google Assistant, Amazon Alexa, Siri; you more or less know that these assistants are based on AI.

  Now, more and more manufacturers are including AI in their smartphones with big chip manufacturers producing chips with built-in AI capabilities.

  The AI integration is helping in bringing features like scene detection, mixed and virtual reality elements and more and more features.

  AI is going to play a major role in the next coming years.

- **Smart Cars and Drones:** There is a prominent display of AI technology in smart cars and drones.

  Companies like Amazon and Walmart are heavily investing in drone delivery programs for making delivery faster and more effective.

Tesla cars are the example of how the AI is impacting our daily life.

Did you know that all the Tesla cars are connected with each other and the things that your car learns is shared across all the cars?

That means, if you had to take a sudden left-turn on a cross-road, all the Tesla cars will know how to manoeuvre that turn after they are updated. Tesla cars are running in the US.

- **Social Media Feeds :** Every user of the Internet, is tweeting on Twitter, Facebook or Instagram or Snapchat or other social media apps.

  If you are using social media sites or apps, most of your decisions are being impacted by the AI.

  From the feeds that you see in your timeline and the notifications that you receive from these apps; everything is curated by AI.

  AI takes all your past behaviour, web searches, interactions and everything else that you do when you are on these websites.

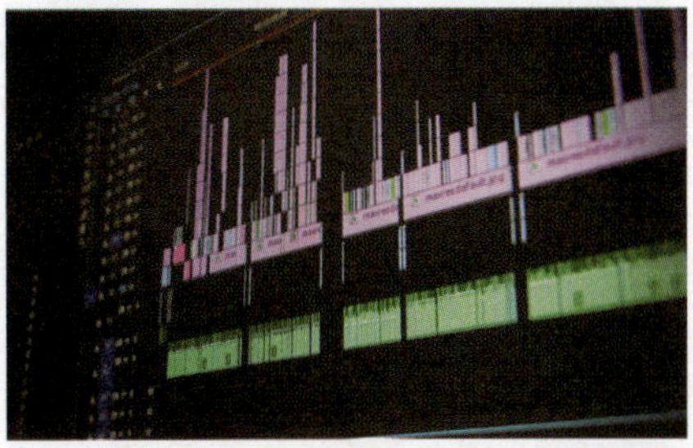

- **Music and Media Streaming Services :** AI impacts our lives through music and various media streaming services that we are using on a daily basis for our entertainment.

  Whether you are using Spotify, Netflix or YouTube; Artificial Intelligence is making the decisions for you in these services.

- **Video Games :** The video game industry is perhaps one of the earliest adopters of AI. Any game that you play has some kind of AI element in it.

  When you are playing games like CS GO, PUBG or Fortnite, you start against a couple of AI-powered bots and then move to play against real players. When you play racing games, you are racing against AI bots.

- **Online Ads Network:** One of the biggest users of artificial intelligence is the online ad industry which uses AI to track user statistics and serves us ads based on those statistics. Without AI, the online advertisement industry will just fail as it would show random ads to the users with no connection to their preferences whatsoever.

  Therefore, next time when you are going online and seeing advertisements or product recommendation, know that AI is impacting your life.

- **Navigation and Travel :** Whether you are using Google or Apple Maps for navigating or calling an Uber or booking a flight ticket, you are using AI. Both Google and Apple use artificial intelligence to interpret thousands of data points that they receive to give you real-time traffic data. When you are calling an Uber or OLA taxi, both the pricing and the car that matches your ride request is decided by the AI.

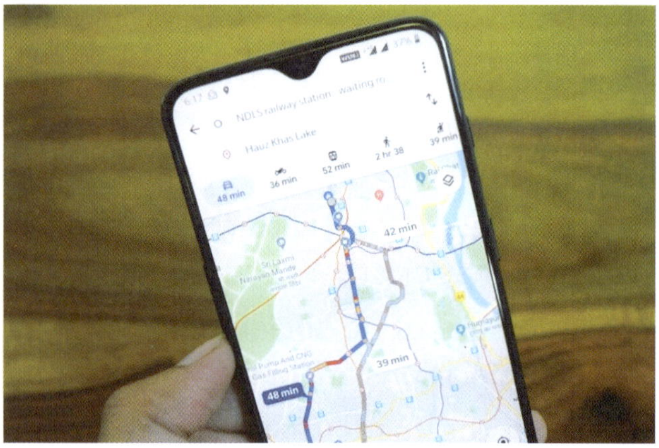

- **Banking and Finance :** Banking and finance industry heavily relies on artificial intelligence for many areas like customer service, fraud protection, investment, etc.

  A simple example is the automated email that you receive from banks from time to time.

  AI is also being trained to look at large samples of fraud data and find a pattern so that you can be warned well before it happens to you. AI can safeguard your interests.

  Chat bots, powered by natural language processing, can serve banking customers quickly and efficiently by answering common queries and providing information promptly.

  Fraud detection is an important application of AI in financial sector.

For Example:

Master Card uses Decision Intelligence technology to analyse various data points to detect fraudulent transactions.

- **Security and Surveillance :** Surveillance system uses AI. It is not possible for human to keep monitoring multiple monitors with feeds from hundreds of cameras at the same time.

  Therefore, using AI makes perfect sense. With technologies like object recognition and facial recognition getting better and better every day, it would not be long when all the security camera feeds would be monitored by an AI and not a human.

ARTIFICIAL INTELLIGENCE: THE PRESENT AND THE FUTURE

As you can see, all of our lives are impacted by artificial intelligence on a daily basis. Whether we are using our smartphones, surfing the Internet, buying products online, using navigation, wasting time on social media or listening to songs on our favourite music streaming service, AI is impacting our choices in one way or another.

DOMAINS OF AI

There are three domains of artificial intelligence.

- Data
- Computer Vision
- Natural Language Processing.

Data

The lifeline of machine learning is *data*. Without data, we cannot train our machines.

Data can be a piece of information or plain facts and statistics collected together for analysis. Whenever we want an AI project to be able to predict an output, we need to train it first using adequate data.

Types of Data

- **Textual Data:** It is collected by input devices like keyboards, scanners or digital documents. Textual data is organized into characters, words, sentences and concepts. *Natural language processing (NLP) is its corresponding AI technology.*

- **Numerical Data:** This type of data is made up of figures and measurements gathered by machines, sensors or people.
- **Visual Data:** It is captured by cameras. It is the data containing images that are tagged according to their contents (people, vehicles, characters, colours, quality, etc.). *Computer Vision (CV) is the corresponding AI technology for visual data.*
- **Audio Data:** This data contains voice or sound. The audio data is stored in digital form in computer using audio formats. *Natural language processing (NLP) is its corresponding AI technology.*
- **Video Data:** This data contains motion pictures. This data is also stored in digital form in computer. *Computer Vision (CV) is the corresponding AI technology for video data.*

  First, we need to specify data requirements. The requirement of data varies with every project. The following questions are related with the data requirement:

  - What data will we need?
  - What format will that data be in?
  - Where will the data come from?
  - What are the compliance requirements of the data source?
  - How often will we need the data?
  - Who is responsible for maintaining the data?
  - What security measures will we need?
  - How will the data be used?
  - What, if any data, will be published or made available?

Once you have specified data requirements, you need to set up data collection. This stage requires the help of people like developers, data architects, database administrators to extract data from the organization.

AI works by combining large volume of data with fast, iterative processing and intelligent algorithms. It allows the software to learn automatically from the patterns in the data. AI is a broad field of study that includes many theories, mathematical methods and technologies.

For Example:

If you want to make an Artificially Intelligent system which can predict the salary of an employee based on his previous salaries, you would feed the data of his previous salaries into the machine. On this data the machine can be trained and it would be able to predict the salary. The old salary data is known as Training Data while the next salary prediction data set is known as the Testing Data.

For better efficiency and results of an AI project, the Training data needs to be relevant and authentic.

If the training data is not accurate (authentic), the machine would not be able to predict the things.

For greater efficiency of the AI project and to find the accurate results, the training data should be authentic and relevant to the problem.

Data Features

Look at your problem once again and try to find the data features required to address this issue. Data features refer to the type of data you want to collect for problem solving. In our salary prediction example, data features would be:

- Basic Salary
- Increment Amount
- Increment Period
- Bonus
- Dearness Allowance
- House Rent Allowance
- Any Other Allowance
- Loan Deductions, etc.

Data Collection

Data can be acquired from various sources. Data plays an important role in an AI project as it creates the base on which the AI project is built. Therefore, the data acquired should be authentic, reliable and correct to get proper results.

Also, the data-acquisition methods should be authentic so that our project does not create any sort of conflicts with anyone.

After mentioning the Data features, you should know what sort of data is to be collected.

There are various ways in which you can collect data.

Surveys	Web Scraping
Sensors	Cameras
Observations	API (Application Program Interface)

Most of the times, you connect to the Internet and try to acquire data for your project from some random websites. Such data might not be authentic as its accuracy cannot be checked and proved. It becomes necessary to find a reliable source of data to obtain authentic information.

We should also keep in mind that the data which we collect, is open-sourced and does not have any copyright. Extracting private data can be an offence. One of the most trusted sources of information, are the open-sourced websites hosted by the Government. These Government portals have general information on various schemes, laws, etc., in suitable format which can be downloaded and used freely.

Computer Vision

Computer Vision (CV) is defined as a field of study that seeks to develop techniques to enable computers and systems to "see" and derive meaningful information from digital images such as photographs, videos and other visual inputs.

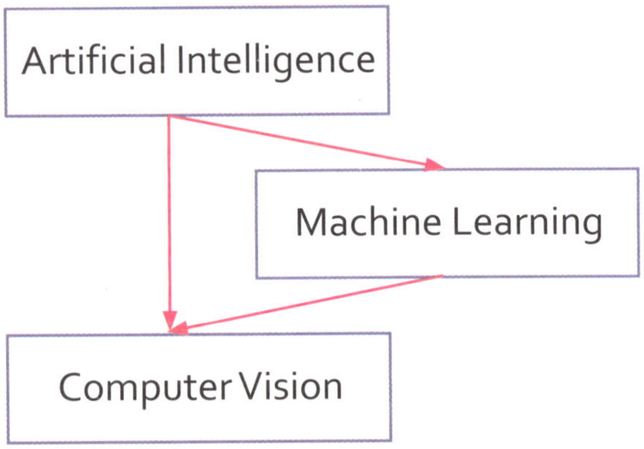

Computer vision is a field of study that focuses on the problem of helping computers to see.

The goal of computer vision is to use the observed image data to infer something from it.

Computer vision relies on pattern recognition and deep learning to recognize what is there in a picture or video. When machines process, analyse and understand images, they can capture images as well as videos in real time and interpret their surroundings.

It is a multidisciplinary field of artificial intelligence and machine learning. It may involve the use of specialized methods and make use of general learning algorithms.

Desire for Computers to See

The modern age of technology is dealing with images and videos. Smartphones have cameras and taking a photo or video and sharing it has become very easier.

There is growth of modern social networks like WhatsApp, Instagram, Twitter (now called X), etc., and these platforms deal with images. People are forgetting the ordinary cameras.

YouTube is the second largest search engine and hundreds of hours of video are uploaded every minute and billions of videos are watched every day.

The Internet is comprised of text and images. Dealing with text on the Internet is bit easy but for images, there is need of algorithms to know what the images contain.

To draw information from image data, we need computers to see an image and understand the content.

- A person can describe the content of a photograph he has seen once.
- A person can summarize a video that he has seen only once.
- A person can recognize a face that he has only seen once before.

We require at least the same capabilities from computers in order to unlock our images and videos.

The goal of computer vision is to understand the content of digital images.

Understanding the content of digital images may involve extracting a description from the image. The description may be:

- an object
- a text description
- a three-dimensional model and so on.

Computer vision is the automated extraction of information from a number of images. Information may be 3D models, camera position, object detection and grouping and searching image content.

Computer Vision and Image Processing

Computer vision is distinct from image processing.

Image processing is defined as the process of creating a new image from an existing image. It is simplifying or enhancing the content in some way. It is a type of digital signal processing.

Examples of image processing include:

- Normalizing properties of the image, such as brightness or colour.
- Cropping the bounds of the image, such as cantering an object in a photograph.
- Removing digital noise from an image of low light level.

Tasks in Computer Vision

A list of some high-level problems where computer vision has been very successful is given below:

- Optical character recognition (OCR)
- Retail
- Medical imaging
- Match move
- Surveillance
- Machine inspection
- 3D model building
- Automotive safety
- Motion capture
- Fingerprint recognition and biometrics

Computer vision has a variety of applications like mobile robot navigation, industrial inspection and military intelligence, human computer interaction, image retrieval in digital libraries, medical image analysis and the realistic production of scenes in computer graphics.

Natural Language Processing (NLP)

Natural language processing is the ability of computers to analyse, understand and generate human language and speech. The next stage of NLP is natural language interaction, which allows human to communicate with computers using normal, everyday language for performing different tasks.

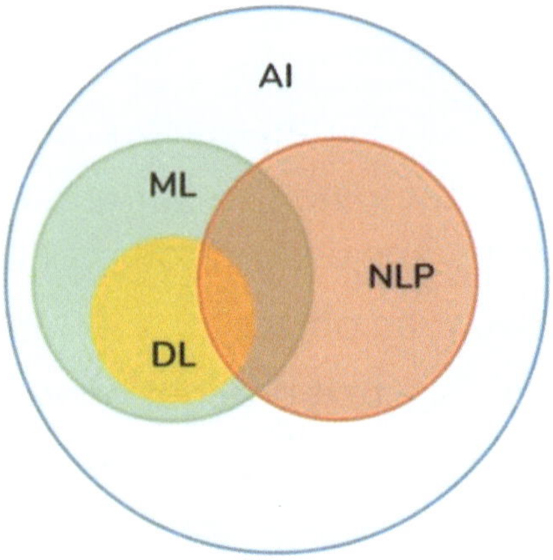

If you have a lot of data written in plain text and you want to automatically get some insights from it, you need to use NLP techniques. These insights could be sentiment analysis, information extraction, information retrieval, search, etc.

One very useful technique, i.e., Optical Character Recognition (OCR) uses NLP.

Optical character recognition (OCR) technology is used for automating data extraction from printed or written text from a scanned document or image file and then converting the text into a machine-readable form.

Subsets of NLP

Natural Language Processing (NLP) has two subsets:

- Natural Language Understanding (NLU)
- Natural Language Generation (NLG)
- **Natural Language Understanding (NLU):** Natural language understanding covers machine reading (reading of raw and unstructured text). NLU helps machines in understanding spoken or written human language.

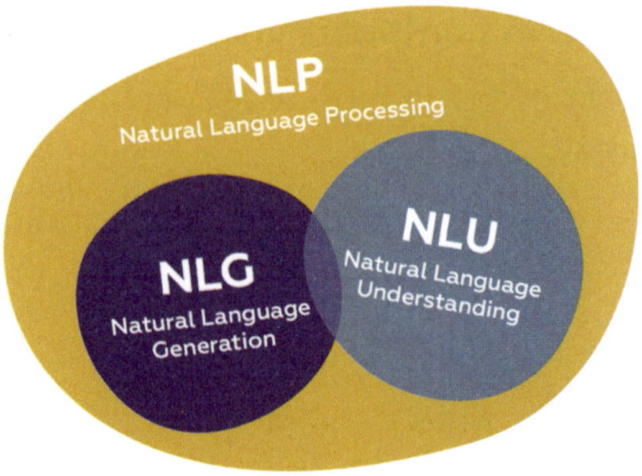

- **Natural Language Generation (NLG):** Natural-language generation converts structured data into natural language. NLG is the process of producing words, phrases and sentences that have contextual meaning and could be understood by humans.

  NLG enables computing devices to generate text and speech from input data. NLG applications have to tackle three stages:

  - **Text Planning:** In this stage, relevant text is fetched from database and ordered in a logical manner.
  - **Sentence Planning:** This stage considers punctuation and text flow, breaking out content into paragraphs and sentences and incorporating pronouns or conjunctions wherever needed.
  - **Realization:** This stage looks into grammatical accuracy, ensuring that rules around punctation and conjugations are followed.

    For Example:

    The past tense of the verb 'see' is 'saw' and not 'seed'.

Advantages of NLP

- A user can ask questions about any subject and get a direct response within seconds from the machine.
- NLP gives exact answers to the question means.
- NLP does not give any unnecessary and unwanted information.
- It helps a machine to communicate with humans in human-language.
- It is very time efficient.

Many companies are using NLP to improve the efficiency in processing of documents, accuracy and identifying the information from large databases.

Applications of NLP

There are a number of applications of NLP.

- **Question Answering:** It focuses on building systems that automatically answer the questions asked by the users in their natural language.
- **Spam Detection:** Spam detection is used to detect unwanted e-mails in the inbox. It deletes spams from inbox and sends it to Spam folder.

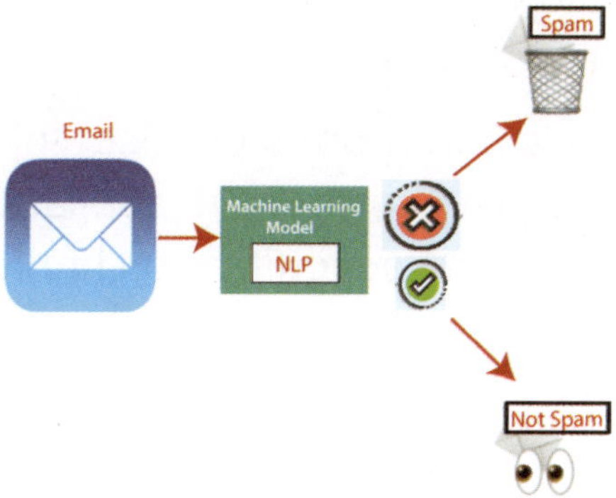

- **Sentiment Analysis:** It is used on the web to analyse the attitude, behaviour and emotional state of the sender.
- **Machine Translation:** It is used in machine translation to translate text or speech from one natural language to another natural language.
- **Spelling Correction:** It helps in spelling correction in the documents.
- **Speech Recognition:** Speech recognition converts the spoken words into text. It is used in applications like mobile, home automation, dictating to a word processor, voice biometrics, voice user interface, etc.
- **Chatbot:** Chatbot is an important application of NLP. It is used by many companies to provide solutions to the queries of customers.

ACTIVITY

MAKE YOUR OWN SMART AI CHATBOT USING SPEECH RECOGNITION

PictoBlox is a Scratch-based graphical programming software. Its user-friendly interface and provides drag-and-drop functionality like Scratch programming language.

PictoBlox only requires to focus on the problem at hand and develop skills such as logical reasoning and problem-solving.

You can prepare many projects on NLP in school lab or at home on your laptop or desktop.

The software can be downloaded from the link:

https://thestempedia.com/product/pictoblox/download-pictoblox/

Scan code:

They have readymade projects related to Artificial Intelligence.

For Example:

A smart home project. In this project, you can control the appliances using the Speech Recognition technology.

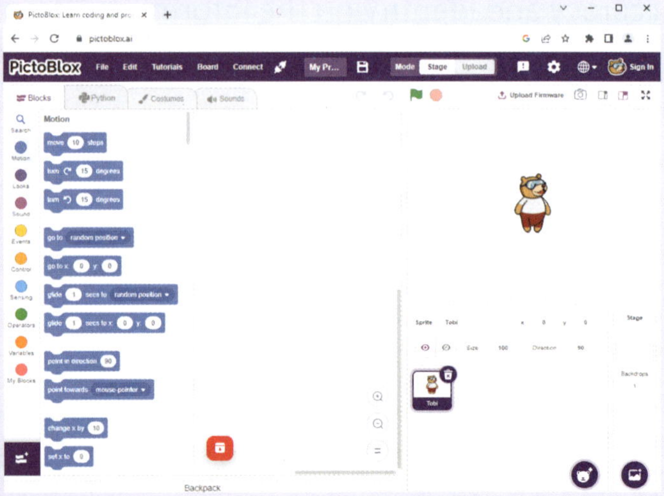

You can build your own project using PictoBlox. It provides you various blocks of commands like:

say, broadcast (with Radio On or Off), sound, move. You can use these blocks for your project. If you have already studied Scratch programming language in any previous class, you will feel at ease in preparing your project.

You must have used a chatbot at least once to ask a question on a website or maybe just to have fun.

In this project, you will first enter a few questions and their answers. Then, when the chatbot runs, it will recognize your speech and convert it into text using PictoBlox's Speech Recognition Extension and then answer your questions accordingly.

You can look for the project using the link:

https://thestempedia.com/project/make-your-own-smart-ai-chatbot-using-speech-recognition/

Scan code:

ACTIVITY

STRANGE POSTER GENERATOR

DESCRIPTION

The Strange Poster Generator uses AI image recognition and transforms the image uploaded in the system, into a Stranger Things poster.

The game can be played using the link: http://evenstranger.pw/ Scan code:

Suppose, you have the given picture.

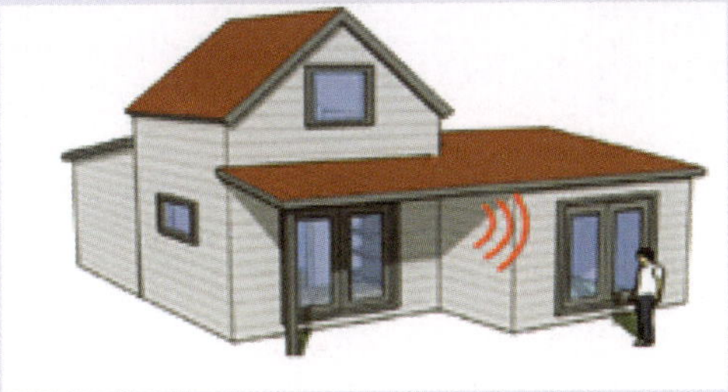

Click UPLOAD AN IMAGE to upload the photo.

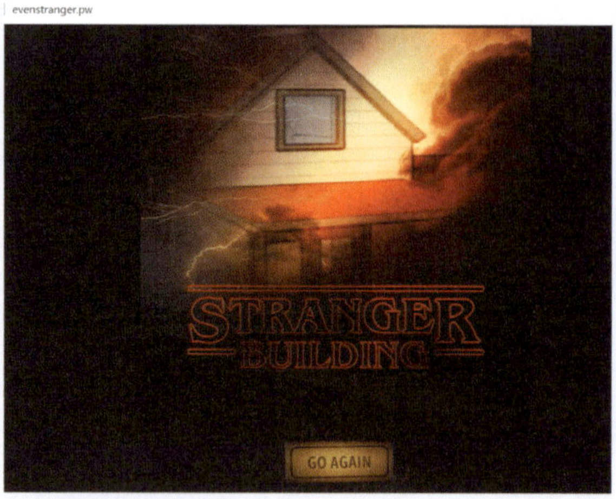

After uploading the photo, it shows you the result.

You can draw your own drawings, cartoons and other objects and load them by clicking GO AGAIN button.

Keep trying!

ACTIVITY

MAGIC SKETCHPAD

DESCRIPTION

This activity is based on machine learning. You have to draw an object without lifting the pen. When you lift the pen, machine tries to finish that stroke and matches the category you have selected. There are multiple categories for objects. Here in the following pictures, we have used the Bucket category and when you draw a simple drawing, magic sketchpad gives it finishing touch.

The game can be played using the link: https://magic-sketchpad.glitch.me/

Scan code:

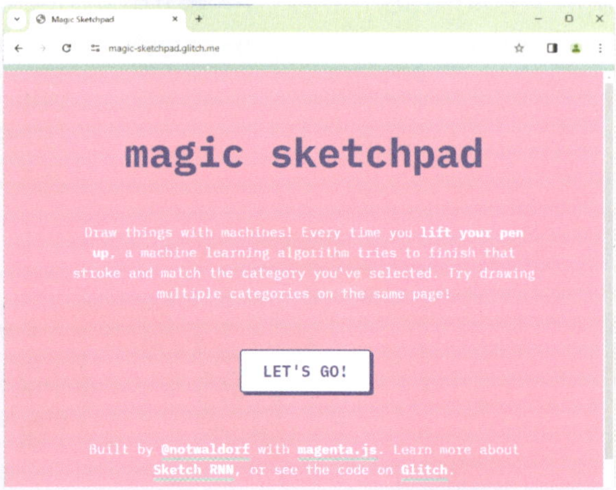

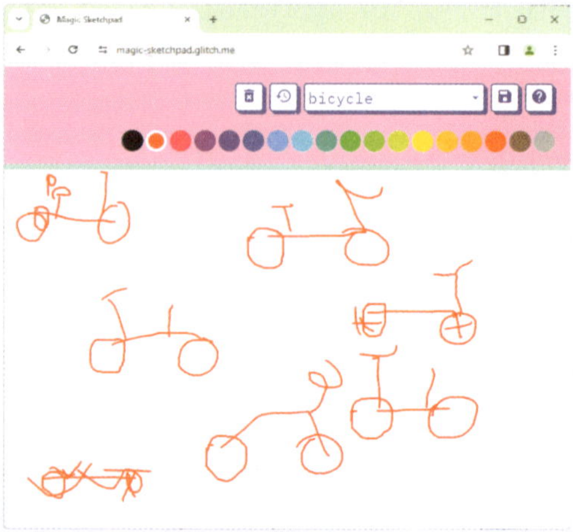

ASSESSMENT FOR ANALYSING PROGRESS TOWARDS ACQUIRED AI-READINESS SKILLS

Machine learning and artificial intelligence are the words most talked today. Various companies, educational institutions, financial institutions are eager to adopt the AI technology but the question is – "Are they ready for the use of AI?"

Artificial intelligence has important effects on business operations of the companies. With the increasing use of AI even small organizations are moving for the use of AI. Non-tech Indian companies are also running the race to streamline artificial intelligence for accelerating the way of their working. Companies are adopting machine learning, big data and especially, AI-powered chatbots to bring a tech-friendly environment in their working environment.

SKILLS REQUIRED FOR FUTURISTIC JOB OPPORTUNITIES

New technologies are emerging day-by-day.

We have never been more globally connected than we are today.

New jobs, skills and mindsets are emerging to succeed over the unpredictable future.

Required skills are:

- **Analyst:** Artificial intelligence and robotics will have a major impact on the future of work, putting business analysts in a great demand. These business forecasters can help companies make informed business decisions and they can play a big role in greater use of artificial intelligence.
- **Banking and Finance:** In the present technological age, banking and finance professionals will be the innovators to lead businesses into the future. A good understanding of technology such as blockchain, crypto-currencies and digital reality will be required to lead the banking and finance world into the new age.
- **Communications:** Automation, digital platforms and other innovations are changing the basic nature of work, putting greater emphasis on the importance of strong communication skills.
- **Knowledge-intensive Jobs:** Future jobs will be knowledge-intensive. Such knowledge-intensive roles give well-educated people an opportunity to contribute to their employer in more effective way.
- **Networking (Communicating):** The ability to network (communicate) effectively will continue to be one of the most essential personal skills for business persons. Knowing how to communicate, inspire and unite ideas contributed by others can open doors in any industry you have to work in.
- **Robotics:** Chatbots that foster human connections have made it into companies and are already allowing banks and large organisations to use technology to innovate and create greater efficiencies.

ACTIVITY

THING TRANSLATOR

MACHINE LEARNING AI MODEL

This experiment takes a picture of something and says it in a different language (SPANISH, HINDI and many more).

You can run the experiment by using the link:

https://experiments.withgoogle.com/thing-translator **Scan code:**

The experiment uses camera of your computer and you have to show you an object and click the picture.

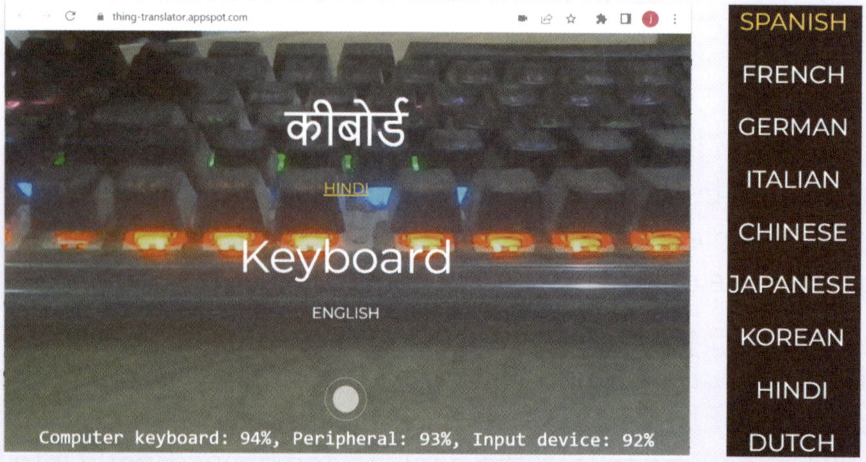

In this picture, a keyboard has been shown to the experiment and it has spoken the name Keyboard in Hindi and English both. (We have selected HINDI language for translation).

ACTIVITY

GAME OF CHANCE

ROCK, PAPER, SCISSORS

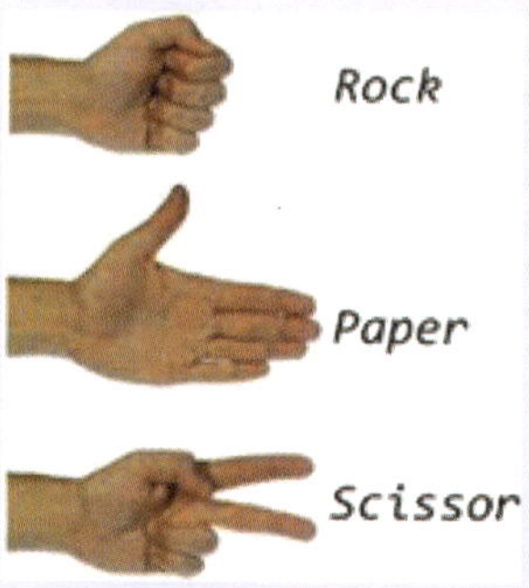

The familiar game of Rock, Paper, Scissors is played in the following manner:

At the same time, two players display one of three shapes of hand: a Rock, Paper or Scissors.

- → To play Rock, simply ball your hand into a fist.
- → To play Paper, extend your palm with your fingers outstretched.
- → To play Scissors, use two fingers to mimic the shape of an open pair of scissors.

A Rock beats Scissors, Scissors beat Paper by cutting it and Paper beats Rock by covering it.

Rock, paper, scissors is an example of a zero-sum game without perfect information. Whenever one player wins, the other loses.

You can play this game through the website:

https://www.twoplayergames.org/game/rock-paper-scissors

Scan code:

How does a Computer Think?

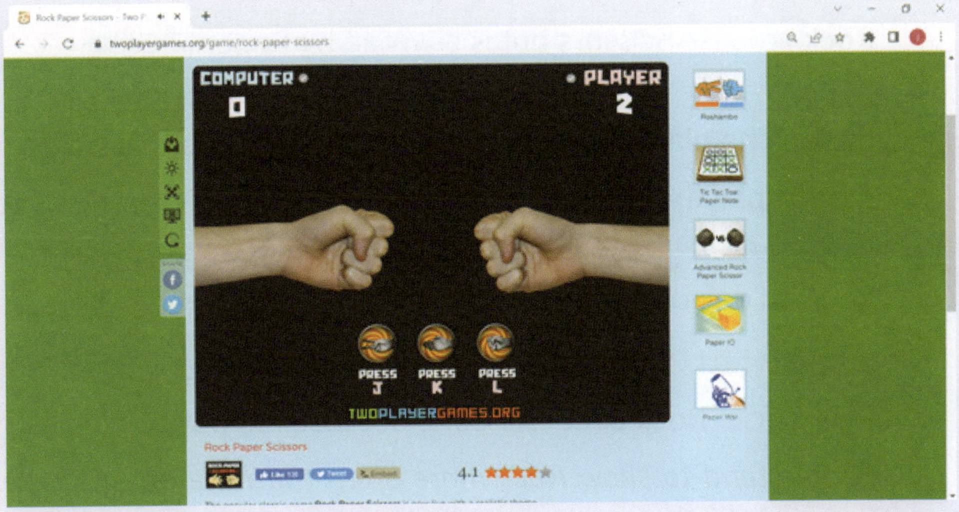

Hey! I am a computer. I am trying to predict your moves based on your history because you are very likely to repeat yourself.

I keep track of the conditional probabilities of your picking each of the three objects you last picked.

People find it quite hard to pick a sequence of perfectly random choices. Therefore, any pattern that a player develops could be learned by the opponent and used to win the game.

As you play, I learn the pattern of objects that you are most likely to pick.

Even when you are actively trying to beat me, your choices will ultimately repeat themselves and all I have to do is identify patterns within the data. The more hands you play – the more data I have – the better I will be at predicting your behaviour and beating you. Do not believe me? Keep playing!

Simple Explanation of Rock, Paper, Scissors Game

In the Rock, Papers and Scissors game, the players show their shape of hand on the count of three.

You can also count down by saying "Rock, Paper, Scissors, shoot...........!" On the word "shoot," both players reveal the object they chose.

- **Play one of the three objects against your opponent.**

  You and your opponent will each form one of the three objects—either Rock, Paper or Scissors.

  Both players must throw at the same time. If one player delays, the result is not fair and you should start the game again.

  Do not play the same object every time. Change it to fool your opponent.

- Determine the winner.

  Each object wins against one shape and loses to another.

- Rock crushes Scissors but is covered by Paper.
- Paper covers rock but is cut by Scissors and Scissors is crushed by Rock but cuts paper. The player who picks the stronger of the two objects is the winner.
- If both players show the same object, it is a tie. In this situation, play again until there is a clear winner.
- You can decide on how many rounds of the game will be played.

Choosing which Item to Show

- Play Rock. Rock beats scissors, but loses to paper.

  People tend to show Rock more often than the other shapes, especially if they are inexperienced.

  Try to predict your opponent's next move by paying attention to their patterns.

- Play Paper. Paper wins against Rock, but loses to Scissors.

  Paper is a good object to show if you are undecided because there is a bigger chance that your opponent will play Rock than Scissors.

- Play Scissors. Scissors has an advantage over Paper but can be beaten by Rock.

  If you find yourself losing when you show Rock, switch to Scissors. This will help you overcome an opponent who relies on Paper.

  An opponent who discovers your strategy can easily beat you. If you are able to determine or discover the strategy of the computer, you can beat the computer.

ACTIVITY

GAME 1

MYSTERY ANIMAL (BASED ON NATURAL LANGUAGE PROCESSING - NLP)

Mystery Animal is a new spin on the classic 20-questions game. The computer pretends to be an animal and you have to guess what it is using your voice. Ask any yes-or-no question you want, like "Do you have feathers?" or "Do you sleep at night?" Play it on a Google Home by saying "Hey Google, talk to Mystery Animal," or try it on the site.

Mystery Animal is a Voice Experiment that lets you play a guessing game where the computer pretends to be an animal and you have to guess what it is.

You can play this game through the website:

https://mysteryanimal.withgoogle.com

Scan code:

Playing Mystery Animal

You can currently access Google's "Mystery Animal" game in several ways:

Go to the website at: https://mysteryanimal.withgoogle.com/ and click "Preview it here".

- Speak to a Google Home unit and say "OK Google, talk to Mystery Animal".
- Speak to the Google Assistant app on your phone and say "OK Google, talk to Mystery Animal".

Google will now choose a random animal that you need to guess. You can speak aloud to ask a wide range of "Yes" and "No" questions such as:

- Are you a mammal?
- Do you have feathers?
- Do you live underground?
- Do you eat meat?
- Do you live in North America?
- And such...

For each question you ask, Google will answer aloud. Since no typing or reading is needed, this game can work wonderfully with young children as well.

This is a great opportunity for students to work on creating good questions that will help narrow down the animal. You will have 20 "Yes" and "No" questions to try to determine what the mystery animal is. If you do not, Google will let you know what the animal was in the end.

Classroom Uses

- As mentioned before, this "Mystery Animal" game is a great way to teach questioning skills and critical thinking skills.
- Additionally, this activity can also fit in perfectly in your science class as it covers a large number of organisms, their characteristics and biology vocabulary.
- Beyond that, this can also be a neat way to demonstrate the power of artificial intelligence, since it is Google's machine learning and knowledge graph that is interpreting your questions and coming back with an answer.
- Finally, students can play the game on their own or they can work together as a group or the entire class, which gives them a chance to develop social skills, as they learn to work as a group, agree on questions and communicate clearly.

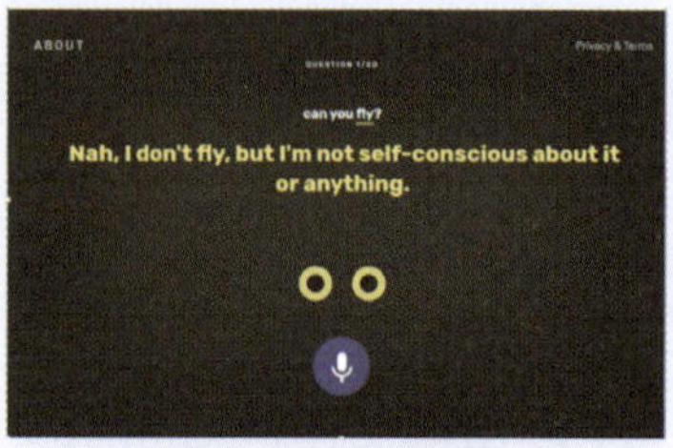

GAME 2

EMOJI SCAVENGER HUNT (BASED ON COMPUTER VISION - CV)

Emoji Scavenger Hunt is an experiment that leverages the power of neural networks and your phone's camera to identify the real-world versions of the emojis we use every day.

Emoji Scavenger Hunt is a fun experimental game where you are shown an emoji and you have a set number of seconds to find the real-world equivalent object and point your phone camera at it, extending your timer. As you play and find emojis in the real world, the subsequent emojis shown increase in difficulty. Starting out with objects you are likely to have on hand like a shoe, book or your own hand and progressing to things like a banana, a candle or even a scooter.

To play the game, you need to visit this website:

https://emojiscavengerhunt.withgoogle.com/ Scan code:

Note that the game only works on mobile devices, not on the desktop. Give the website permission to access your camera. The first scavenger hunt is pretty easy, say it will ask you to find things that look like your keyboard or mouse, which can be found in your vicinity easily. You can also share your scores on social networking platforms like Twitter and Facebook.

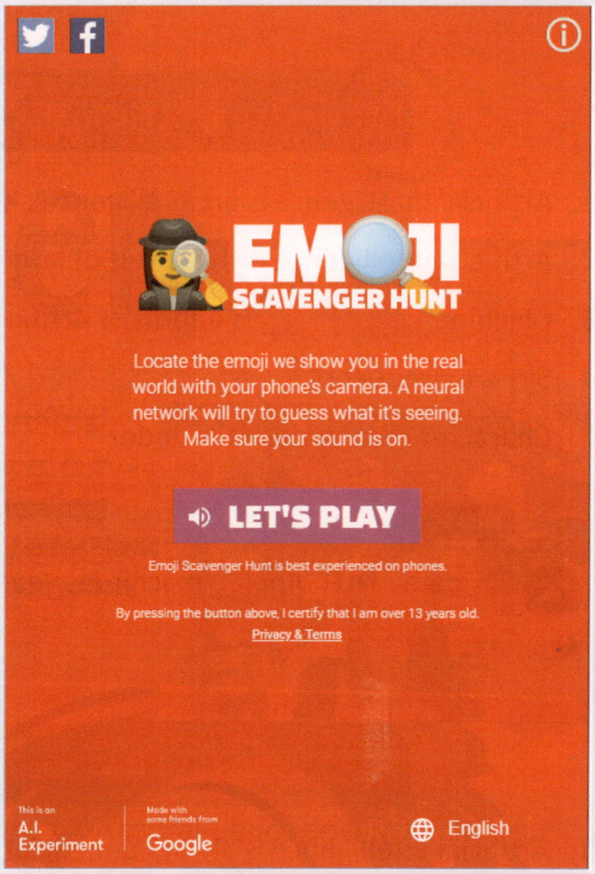

"Locate the emoji we show you in the real world with your phone's camera. A neural network will try to guess what it is seeing. Make sure your sound is on," says Google on its website.

Google makes it clear that it does not store any images on its servers. "All the interactions are happening locally on your device," added Google.

Emojis have become a language all their own, so much so that we use them every day to communicate in texts and emails. These emojis are obviously modelled after their real-world counterparts, which got us thinking: can we use the power of our phones to find the real-world versions of the emojis we use every day?

It works like this: the game will show you an emoji and you have to find its real-world version before time expires. While you search, the neural network will try and guess what it is seeing—proof that machine learning can be used for more than serious applications.

The rules are simple. You will be shown an emoji on the screen and you have to find its real-life variant in a given time. So, if the game shows you a pen emoji, you need to find a pen. Successfully finding an object unlocks the next one and so on. Google says that the game is designed to help train their emoji machine learning algorithms better.

EXERCISE

Performance Assessment, Review and Analysis

Fill in the Blanks with Given Hints

1. Artificial Intelligence is an intelligence shown by ___________ .
2. Artificial intelligence is the result of larger ___________.
3. Machine ___________ is a form of Artificial Intelligence.
4. Siri is a product of ___________ .
5. Character recognition falls under ___________.

HINTS

data, NLP, Apple, machines, learning

Write T for True and F for False

1. Artificial Intelligence is always beneficial. [ ]
2. Artificial Intelligence is a superset of machine learning. [ ]
3. Neural network is a subset of Artificial Intelligence. [ ]
4. Google Doc can be used as Story Speaker. [ ]
5. Artificial intelligence is possessed by humans. [ ]
6. Artificial Intelligence is a branch of Natural Language Processing. [ ]
7. Computer Vision is related with images and videos. [ ]
8. Image is not a type of data. [ ]
9. OCR stands for Output Character Recognition. [ ]
10. Narrow Artificial Intelligence cannot do any intelligent thing. [ ]
11. Natural language processing has two subsets and natural language generation is one of them. [ ]
12. A robot is used to lift a block of metal. It is an example of artificial super intelligence. [ ]

Multiple Choice Questions

Tick the best alternatives.

1. Which one of the following is an application of AI?
   (a) Remote Controlled Drone
   (b) Self-Driving Car
   (c) Automated Teller Machine in a Bank
   (d) Printing Press
2. This language is easy to learn and is one of the most popular language for AI today is ______.
   (a) C++ (b) Python
   (c) Java (d) PASCAL
3. What does NLP stand for in AI?
   (a) Neutral Learning Projection (b) Neuro-Linguistic Programming
   (c) Natural Language Processing (d) Neural Logic Presentation
4. What is Artificial Intelligence?
   (a) Code people created (b) Robots that are smarter than us
   (c) Robots that act like human being (d) Fake intelligence
5. What is AI used for?
   (a) Healthcare (b) Education
   (c) Transportation (d) All of these
6. Which are the examples of AI in daily life?
   (a) Virtual Characters (Hologram, etc.) (b) Siri
   (c) Regular Vacuum (d) Amazon Alexa
7. Which of the following is not a goal or feature of AI?
   (a) Learning (b) Perception
   (c) Creating Art (d) Moving and manipulating objects

8. Which one of these jobs could not be taken by a robot with AI? (at least this century)
   (a) Bank Clerk
   (b) Shop worker
   (c) Telephone sales person
   (d) Doctor
9. Which of these does not use machine learning/AI?
   (a) Siri/Alexa
   (b) Face recognition on your phone
   (c) Self-driven Car
   (d) Wireless Speaker
10. Which of these is not an AI technology?
    (a) Animation
    (b) Facial Recognition
    (c) Robotics
    (d) Image recognition
11. Which of these jobs could be taken by a robot using AI?
    (a) Nurse
    (b) Doctor
    (c) Bank Clerk
    (d) Teacher
12. Which of the following is not a domain of Artificial Intelligence?
    (a) Compute Vision
    (b) Data
    (c) NLP
    (d) All are domains of AI
13. What does NLP stand for in AI?
    (a) Neutral Learning Projection
    (b) Neuro-Linguistic Programming
    (c) Natural Language Processing
    (d) Neural Logic Presentation
14. Which of the following is not a type of AI?
    (a) ANI
    (b) AGI
    (c) ASI
    (d) AFI
15. Siri is a product of ________________.
    (a) Google
    (b) Apple
    (c) Amazon
    (d) Paytm
16. Alexa is a product of ________________ .
    (a) Google
    (b) Apple
    (c) Amazon
    (d) Paytm
17. Self-driving car is an example of ________________.
    (a) Artificial General Intelligence
    (b) Weak Artificial Intelligence
    (c) Artificial Super Intelligence
    (d) Broad Artificial Intelligence

18. Self-driving car is an example of ________________ .

(a) Computer Intelligence [ ] (b) Data Science [ ]

(c) Computer Vision [ ] (d) Natural Language Processing [ ]

19. On a road toll collection barrier, which of the following activity is the correct option?

(a) Computer Vision [ ] (b) Data Science [ ]

(c) Natural Data Processing [ ] (d) Note counting [ ]

20. Read the given statements and select the correct answer from the given options.

Statement 1. All the elements of Artificial Intelligence are interconnected.

Statement 2. When an element from an AI-based project is removed, there will be imbalance in the project.

(a) Both the statements are true [ ]

(b) Both the statements are false [ ]

(c) Statement 1 is true but Statement 2 is false [ ]

(d) Statement 1 is false but Statement 2 is true [ ]

Competency Based Questions

1. Match Column A with Column B Column.

Column A	Column B
1. Expert System	A. Simulate how a human would behave as a conversation partner.
2. Chatbot	B. Uses knowledge stored in a knowledge base but requires the intervention of human expert.
3. Digital Assitant	B. Autonomouse vehicle.
4. Self-driving car	D. Works on verious mobile platforms.

(a) 1 -> B; 2 -> A; 3 -> D; 4 -> C

(b) 1 -> A; 2 -> B; 3 -> C; 4 -> D

(c) 1 -> D; 2 -> A; 3 -> B; 4 -> C

(d) 1 -> C; 2 -> A; 3 -> D; 4 -> B

2. A worker is holding a machine in his hand and he is focusing it on a paper. There is something written on the paper like the characters shown in the following image:

   Explain that Stuff! 0123456789 0

   Which is the name of the technique that is being used to read the characters?

3. Activity: Letter to Future Self

   Imagine the world in 2030 and write a letter to your future self. Be sure to mention things that you think your future self would probably be doing and experiencing in daily life.

   (In the following letter, fill in the blanks (numberings) in with the suitable words or whatever sentences come into your mind)

   Place ____________________

   Date ____________________

   Dear ________(a)__________,

   It feels a little strange to be writing a letter to my future self, but it is also rather exciting!

   At present I am very interested in ________________(1)_____________and am sure this is a hobby that has proved beneficial and I am now a skilled ______(2)__________ ____.

   So tell me, have things changed a lot? Do we still have a lot of __________ (3)_______________?

   Has Artificial Intelligence proved to be ____________(4)_____________?

   You must be so used to ___________(5)______________ while we struggle to _________ (6)_________.

   Is our Pet _____(7)__________ doing well or have you replaced it with _____(8)_________? Ha! Ha! It is so much easier, right?

   How is your preparation for the new job? Must be really nice to be ______ (9)_________________.

   Have you changed the ___________________(10)_________________________?

   I am sure things have turned out well for you in 2030. Great ________ (11)______________________ !

   It has been nice writing to you___________(12)______________________________________.

   Hope this letter brings back old memories.

   Yours sincerely,

   ___________ (b)___________

Answer the Following Questions

1. Define the term artificial intelligence.

2. What are the types of artificial intelligence?

3. What are the application areas of artificial intelligence?

4. What is machine learning?

5. What are the uses of AI in daily activities?

6. What is the difference between voice recognition and speech recognition?

7. What are the applications of AI in the field of banking?

8. What is natural language processing?

9. Write the types of data.

10. What is narrow artificial intelligence?

11. What is Computer Vision?

____

____

12. Write the full forms of the following:

- ANI ____________
- ASI ____________
- NLU ____________
- ML ____________
- DL ____________
- AGI ____________
- NLP ____________
- NLG ____________
- CV ____________
- OCR ____________

LAB ACTIVITY

For Students

- Make a presentation on Artificial Intelligence showing the applications of AI.
- Write how machines are able to give results on the basis of input.
- Mention the use of Artificial Intelligence in biometrics.
- In the given circles, mention the areas where AI is being used.

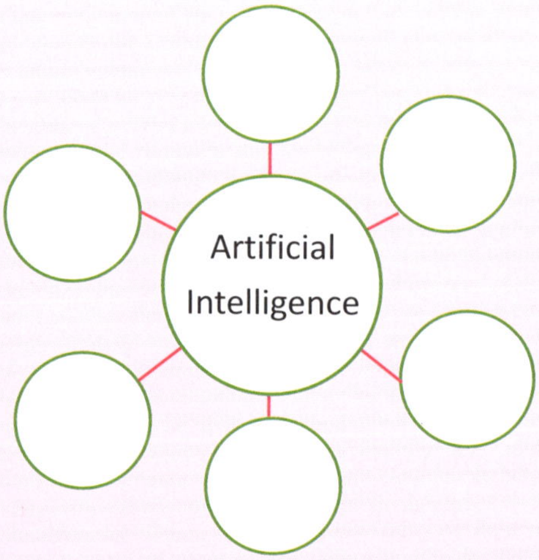

Group Discussion:

Discuss in the group of 4 students:

- What is the use of AI?
- Areas of uses of AI.

For Teachers

- Artificial Intelligence has become the talk in the field of Computer Science. It can create wonders in technology. On the basis of latest developments in the field of AI, explain the students some more uses of AI not covered in the book.

2

RELATE

Introduction

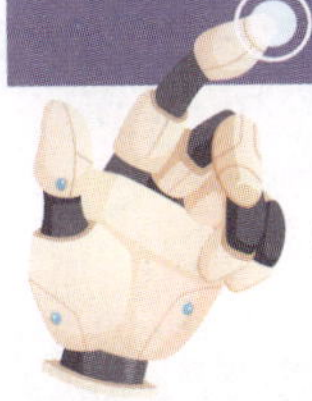

AI has taken wings and has started to fly high. Every day we hear some development in the field of artificial intelligence.

There are various applications of AI, which we are using and experience almost every day.

Even AI can turn your house into AI-powered dream home.

Let us *relate* the applications of AI in our daily lives and study about these applications in details.

Learning Outcomes

- Learners to relate to application of Artificial Intelligence in their daily lives.

Coverage:

To unleash their imagination towards smart homes and build an interactive story around it.

To relate, apply and reflect on the Human-Machine Interactions.

APPLICATIONS OF ARTIFICIAL INTELLIGENCE IN DAILY LIVES

With all the developments in AI from visual recognition, biometrics to self-driving cars, instant machine translation, etc., we can say that AI is making impact on our daily lives from moment to moment.

Sometimes you are using such an application which you do not know is using Artificial Intelligence.

You are most likely using AI on your way to school or work, communicating online with friends, searching on the web and making online purchases.

Let us go through details in which areas AI applications are being used:

Google's AI-Powered Predictions

Using data of a particular location from smartphones, Google Maps (Maps), you can analyse the speed of movement of traffic at any given time.

Maps can suggest the fastest routes to and from your place of destination.

UBER AI

Ride-Sharing Apps Like Uber

You must have travelled by Uber or OLA. Have you thought how do they determine the price of your ride? How do they minimize the wait time once you call for a taxi? How do these services match you with other passengers? The answer to all these questions is Machine Learning.

Commercial Flights Use an AI Autopilot

AI autopilots in commercial airlines is one of the early uses of AI technology.

AI-Driven Vehicles

In the future, AI will shorten your travelling time using self-driving cars.

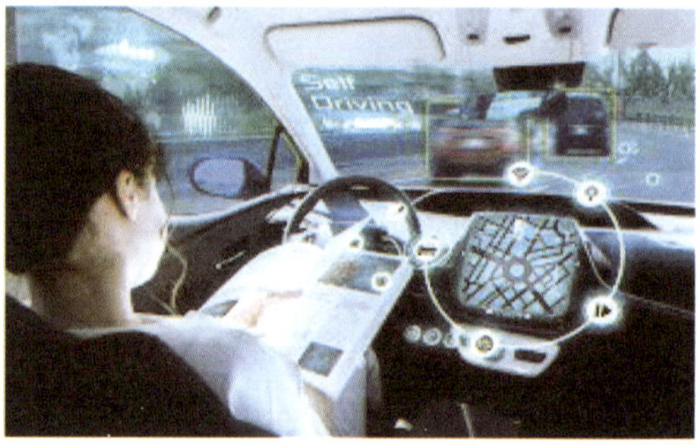

- These self-driven cars result in up to 90% fewer accidents.
- More efficient ride sharing is possible to reduce the number of cars on the road by up to 75%.
- Smart traffic lights that reduce wait times by 40% and overall travel time by 25% in a pilot study.

In Email

- **Spam Filters**

  AI is helpful in emails. In fact, your email inbox is getting AI powers and features like: the spam filter. Simple rules-based filters (*i.e.* "filter out those messages with the words 'prize money' and 'you have won' etc., that come from unknown addresses") are not effective against spam, because spammers can quickly update their messages to work around them.

  Through the use of machine learning algorithms, Gmail successfully filters 99.9% of spam.

- **Smart Email Categorization**

  Gmail uses a similar approach to categorize your emails. It categorizes mails into primary, social and promotion inboxes, as well as labelling emails as important.

Can your inbox reply to emails for you? Google introduced *Smart reply* to Inbox in 2015, a next-generation email interface. *Smart reply* uses machine learning to automatically suggest three different brief responses to answer the email.

In the coming days, smart reply will be able to provide complex responses. Google has already demonstrated its intentions in this area with Allo. Allo is a new instant messaging app which can use smart reply to provide both text and emoji responses.

Grading and Assessment

- **Plagiarism Checkers**

  Plagiarism means taking or copying someone else's work or ideas and passing them off as one's own.

  Many high school and college students are familiar with services like Turnitin, a popular tool used by instructors to analyse students' writing for checking plagiarism.

  Plagiarism detection for regular text like paragraphs, letters, essays, books, etc., relies on a having a massive database of reference materials to compare with the text of student.

  However, Machine Learning can help detect the plagiarizing of sources that are not located within the database; such as sources in foreign languages or older sources that have not been digitized.

  For Example:

  Two researchers used ML to predict, code of the program had been plagiarized. They looked at number of factors that could be unique to each programmer like:

  » average length of code

  » how much each line was indented?

  » how frequent code comments were and so on.

  The algorithmic key to plagiarism is the similarity function. This function outputs a numeric estimate of how similar two documents are.

- **Robo-Readers**

  Giving grading on an essay-writing is a laborious thing. Now, essay-gradings AIs are there.

  In the Graduate Record Exam (GRE), the primary test used for graduate school, grades for essays are given using robo-reader called e-Rater.

There are many areas where AI can improve education in the future. Classes may be replaced by personalized and adaptive learning that suits to each student's individual strength and weaknesses.

ML may also be used to identify students early on so that schools can focus extra resources on those students and decrease dropout rates.

Banking/Personal Finance

- In many banks, financial transactions are heavily dependent on machine learning. Better customer service is being provided by the banks to the customers.
- AI is also used for fraud detection. AI is used to create such systems that learn what types of transactions are suspicious or fraudulent.
- Credit decisions are also done by AI systems. When a person applies for a loan or credit card, the bank can quickly determine whether to accept loan application.

Social Networking

- ### Facebook

When you upload photos on the Facebook, the service automatically highlights faces and suggests friends to tag. How is it able to identify instantly which of your friends is in the photo? Facebook uses AI to recognize faces.

Facebook shows advertisements on its homepage or webpages that are relevant to your interests. Better targeted advertisements mean you are more likely to click them and buy something from the advertisers. When you do any purchase through the link, Facebook gets paid by the advertiser.

Facebook uses DeepText, a text understanding engine that can understand the textual content of several thousand posts per second, spanning more than 20 languages.

DeepText applies Neural Networks to unlabelled data sets of posts and comments to understand their meaning and sentiments. DeepText is also used for automating the removal of spam. It helps popular personalities sort through the millions of comments on their posts to see the most relevant.

- ### Pinterest

Pinterest uses computer vision (CV). You now know that CV is an application of AI where computers are taught to "see," and automatically identify the pins in the images and then recommend visually similar pins.

- **Instagram**

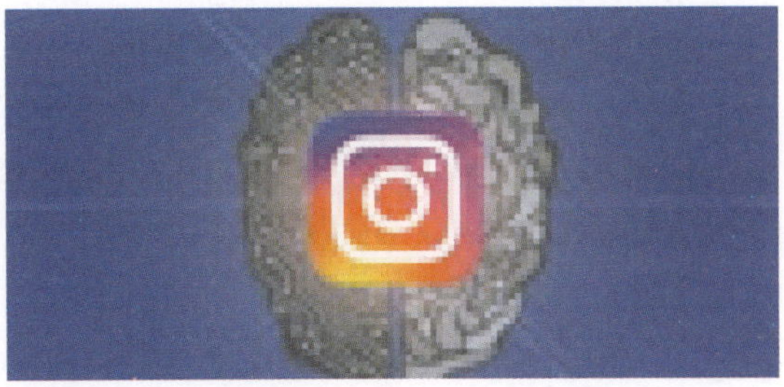

Instagram uses Machine Learning (ML) to the contextual meaning of emoji. By algorithmically identifying the sentiments behind emojis, Instagram can create and auto-suggest emojis and emoji hash-tags.

- **Snapchat**

Snapchat introduced facial filters. These filters track facial movements that allow users to add animated effects or digital masks that adjust when their faces moved.

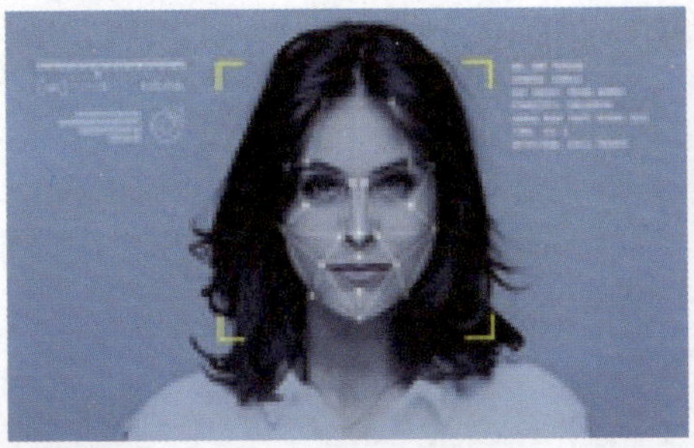

Online Shopping

- **Search**

When you search for a product, *e.g.*, on Amazon, Amazon quickly return a list of the most relevant products related to your search.

The structured data provides them many such relevance features and they learn from past search patterns and adapt to what is important to their customers.

- **Recommendations**

You see recommendations for the products you are interested in.

For Example:

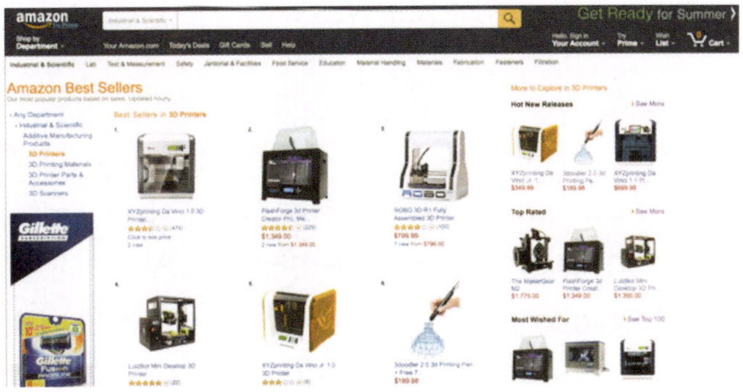

You will see "Customers who viewed this item also viewed" and "Customers who bought this item also bought", etc.

Amazon uses artificial neural networks (ANN) to generate these product recommendations for a particular user.

Mobile Use

- **Voice-To-Text**

A standard feature on smartphones today is voice-to-text. By pressing a button or saying a particular phrase, you can start speaking and your phone converts the audio into text. Google uses artificial neural networks for voice search. Microsoft has developed a speech-recognition system that can transcribe conversation slightly more accurately than humans.

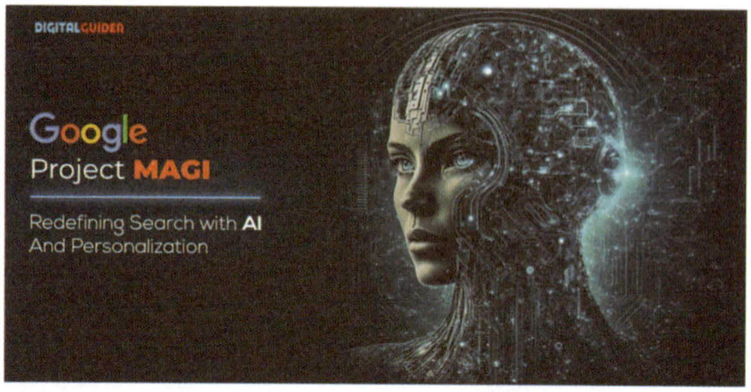

- **Smart Personal Assistants**

Now voice-to-text technology is accurate enough to rely on for basic conversation, it has become the control interface for a new generation of smart personal assistants.

Amazon's Alexa is an AI-powered personal assistant that accepts voice commands to create to-do lists order items online, set reminders and answer questions (using Internet searches).

Echo smart speakers allow you to integrate Alexa into your living room and use voice commands to ask natural language questions, play music order pizza, book an Uber and integrate with smart home devices.

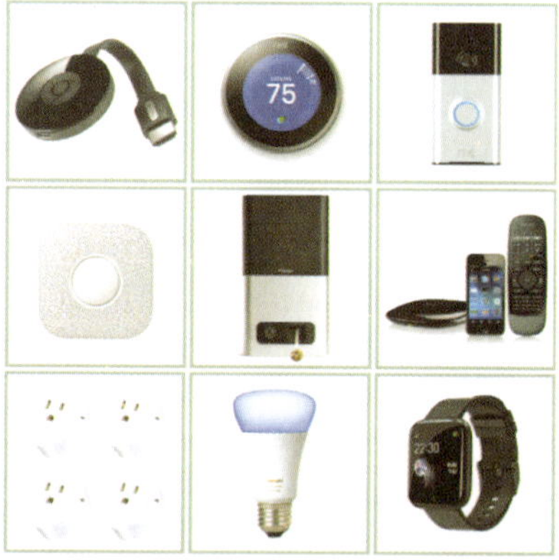

There are variety of devices that can be controlled through Amazon's Alexa.

Microsoft has followed suit with Cortana in Windows 10/Windows 11 its own AI assistant that comes pre-loaded on Windows-based computers and Microsoft smartphones.

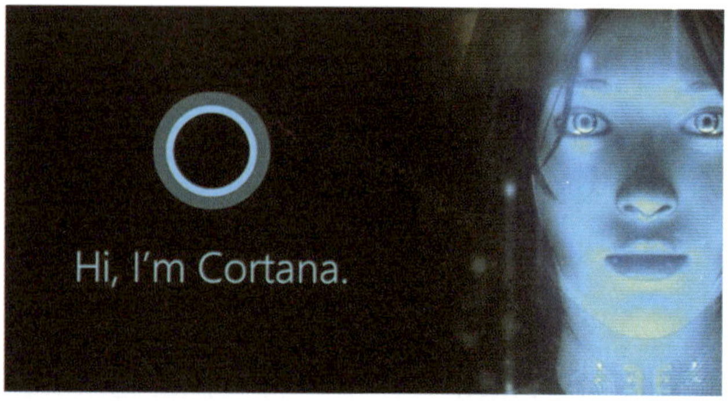

RELEVANCE OF AI IN OUR LIVES

Artificial Intelligence has a great relevance on our lives.

The 6 A's of relevance of AI are:

- AI automates repetitive learning and discovery through data.
- AI augments (adds) intelligence to existing products.
- AI adapts through progressive learning algorithms to let the data do the programming.
- AI analyzes more and deeper data using neural networks that have many hidden layers.

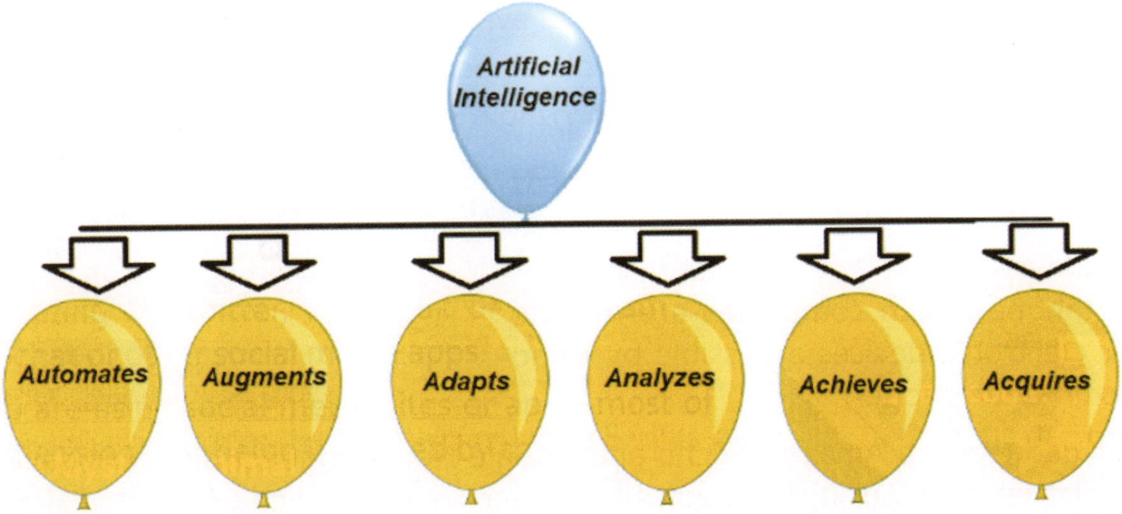

- AI achieves incredible accuracy through deep neural networks.

  For Example:

  Your interactions with Alexa and Google are all based on deep learning. And these products keep getting more accurate the more you use them.
- AI acquires (gets) the most out of data. The answers are in the data. You just have to apply AI to find them.

SMART HOME

AI is dissolving in our lives and even into our home. Now home automation tools have become more affordable, the smart home is within the reach of simple well-to-do people also.

Smart homes save your money and energy consumption.

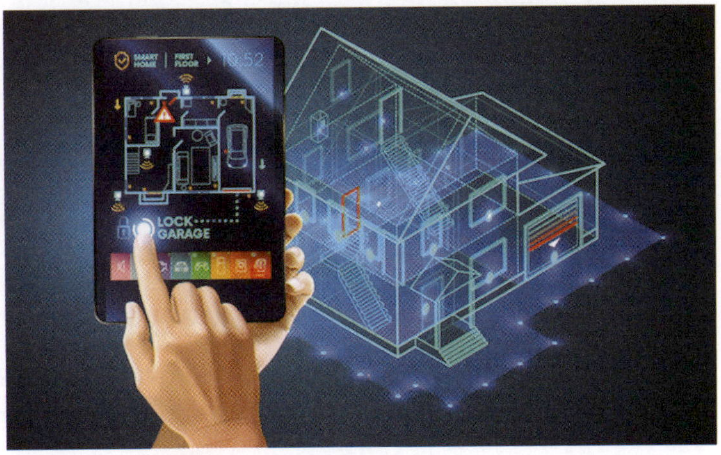

- **AI Integration:** Artificial intelligence (AI) is becoming a powerful factor in technology. It is also dominating the home automation market very fast.

  AI allows us to integrate various smart solutions into our everyday tasks.

  Presence of AI in home automation allows us to:

  - control our appliances
  - secure our homes
  - limit our expenses.

  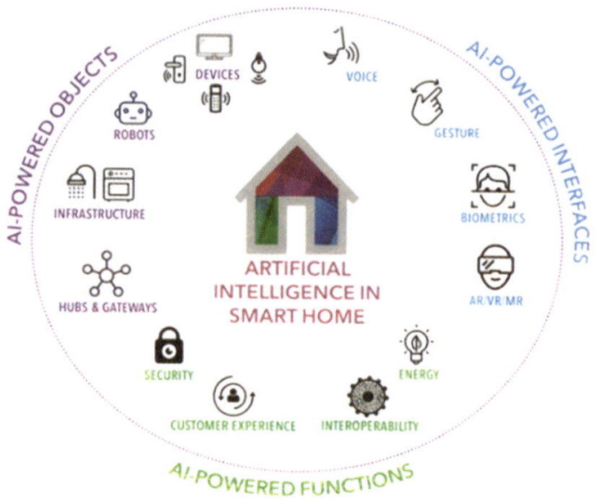

  The main goal of home automation is to limit the need for human functions.

  With the fast advancement in technology and AI, you can expect a lot of changes in the way you live in your home.

  Nowadays, people are addicted to their smartphones. Tech companies are making their electronic devices accessible by using apps on smartphones.

  Now, gadgets like Amazon's Echo and Google Home connect different devices using the Internet of things (IoT) by voice command. This is called Connected Home but AI driven Home is called Smart Home.

AI in Home Automation

Imagine you are going to your home. You are a mile away from home, the Home AI detects your arrival. This starts a series of event like:

- switching your AC from energy saving mode to your preferred temperature
- unlock your doors as you enter the house
- turn on your lights
- play your favourite music or your favourite show on TV.

AI offers simplicity and safety through home automation. Home security is now becoming cheaper and more accessible. Even a normal person can install this technology in homes.

You will be able to control the AI with your voice and this is the some convenient an automatic house can become. This would be very beneficial for an aged and differently abled person who finds it difficult operating all the devices.

With home automation, home security is becoming cheaper and smarter.

How AI-based smart home systems work?

All devices in an AI-powered smart home system should be able to:

- communicate with each other
- continuously acquire new data for further learning.

A truly intelligent smart home device employs the learning system, a system capable of making decisions based on historical and real-time data. It requires little to no user control.

When you leave your room and go to the bathroom or balcony, the system should be able to identify your actions and movements. The system would issue appropriate commands to other devices within the network like:

- To turn off the lights in the room you left.
- Turn on the lights in the room you entered.

The goal of smart home devices is to bring down manual settings almost to zero. Using AI and machine learning, you can minimize the inconvenience and human efforts for all connected home-owners.

Let us have a look at some applications of AI in smart home automation.

Location-Based Smart Devices

Smart home devices can be remotely controlled through smartphone apps. You can make your preferences for auto-manage mode also.

For Example:

When you are approaching your home and are within a given radius, the system can set up your room with your own preference of lights, curtains and AC temperature. These features increase comfort level.

Voice-Enabled Devices

Smart devices can be linked with devices like Google Assistant and Amazon Alexa to provide voice-control options in all home automation systems. Voice technology can be used to:

- control lights
- make voice or video calls
- read news
- place orders
- play music and so on.

This voice-interaction feature can be used during a medical emergency in informing the family and friends for immediate attention.

SMART DEVICES USING ARTIFICIAL INTELLIGENCE						
Amazon Alexa	**Google Nest**	**Apple HomePod**	**Rokid Pebble**	**LG Cloi**	**AlphaGo**	**Watson**

Amazon Alexa is a virtual assistant technology. It was first used in the Amazon Echo smart speaker and the Echo Dot, Echo Studio and Amazon Tap speakers. It is capable of voice interaction, music playback, making to-do lists, setting alarms,	Google Nest, previously named Google Home, is a line of smart speakers developed by Google under the Google Nest brand. sub-scription service. The device enables user to speak voice commands to interact with services through Google Assistant.	The HomePod is a smart speaker developed by Apple Inc. The HomePod was designed to work with the Apple Music	The Pebble is the assistant from tech startup Rokid. The camera can recognize your face and the screen can display additional context and info if you ask it a question.	LG CLOi GuideBot offers a comprehensive variety of services based on autonomous driving and AI, such as information guidance, advertising, and security.	AlphaGo is a computer program that plays the board game Go. It was developed by DeepMind Technologies a subsidiary of Google. Subsequent versions of AlphaGo became increasingly powerful, including a version that competed under the name Master.	Watson is a question-answering computer system capable of answering questions posed in natural language, developed in IBM's DeepQA project by a research team led by principal investigator David Ferrucci. Watson was named

(Cont...)

streaming podcasts, playing audio-books, and providing weather, traffic, sports, and other real-time information.	Both in-house and third-party services are integrated allowing users to listen to music, control playback of videos or photos or receive news updates entirely by voice.					after IBM's founder and first CEO, industrialist Thomas J. Watson.

Smart Security Systems

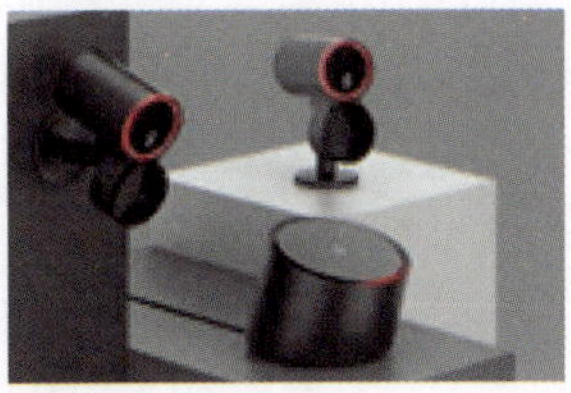

Security systems include:

- facial recognition
- voice recognition
- motion detection
- biometric access control.

- **Facial Recognition:** Smart home devices include Wi-Fi-enabled devices with video capturing security features. You can remotely access these features on your smartphone from any location. Smart systems incorporate facial recognition technology into video cameras that are connected with it.

  AI-based neural networks can identify eyes, nose, chin, etc., of a visitor through the camera and compare with the faces of the home's residents. If the face is not found familiar, the system can send notifications about suspicious activity on the smartphone.
- **Motion Detection:** Motion sensors can detect random movement through video surveillance like detecting intruders and warning home-owners.
- **Voice Recognition:** AI-based voice recognition systems use Natural Language Processing (NLP). This technology isolates voice of person from background noises. It then converts the voice (audio) to a digital file and sends it to the cloud for NLP analysis. It then triggers an appropriate action.

  With machine learning, it is possible to teach a system to recognise a variety of different words or messages.

The term *voice recognition* refers to identifying the speaker rather than meaning of the voice. It can be trained on a specific person's voice or used to verify the identity of the speaker as part of a security process.

- **Biometric Access Control:** Biometric door locks can be integrated into Amazon and Google smart home systems. These usually take photos of the user's fingertips through optical scanners and store them for matching, using fingerprints and passwords.

SMART HOME THINGS

- **Smart Locks:** Smart locks come with keyed and keyless entry systems. They allow you to activate the lock with a code or a key. They alert you in case of any break-in. Locks can be unlocked by using your smartphone. They have Bluetooth or Wi-Fi functionality.
- **Entry Sensors:** Door and window sensors inform you if a door is open. They raise alarm you in the case of a security break.
- **Smart Speaker:** You can listen to your favourite songs in your room. You can also control devices with these smart speakers like Alexa.
- **Smart Cooktops:** They utilise induction technology to heat only the food in your pans. It saves energy, cooks your food faster and prevents heat damage.
- **Smart Home Control Panel:** A smart, touch-screen panel can control lights of your house. Smart control panel detects when you enter the room and lights or AC are turned on.
- **Robotic Technologies:** Vacuum cleaners, window washers can clean your house.
- **Thermostat**: It can maintain a comfortable environment in your house at all times of the day and night.
- **Smoke and Carbon Monoxide Detectors:** Your home automation system can detect smoke and Carbon Monoxide in the air and sound an alarm.
- **Water Leak Detection:** A leak detector can detect a fault of leakage in toilet, beneath a sink and other places.
- **Smart HVAC:** Heating, Ventilation and Air Conditioning system uses smart, wireless technology to communicate with other smart devices and sensors in your house.
- It increases comfort and saves energy.

Optimising Energy Consumption

Smart home automation products provide additional functionality in addition to control. They also optimise energy performance.

With integration of AI and machine learning, smart devices offer energy consumption patterns. On this basis, users can limit the usage of devices and appliances when not required.

If you forgot to turn off a fan or kids went to play outside without switching the AC off, your home system will take care of it.

An AI-Smart Home can reduce your electricity bill and carbon footprint by controlling smart plugs, thermostats and automatic light sensors.

These AI Smart Houses will definitely offer peace of mind to the owner and take care of all the work in the house, but it will cost a lot initially as of now. But with time, we will see everyone owning an AI smart home in the future.

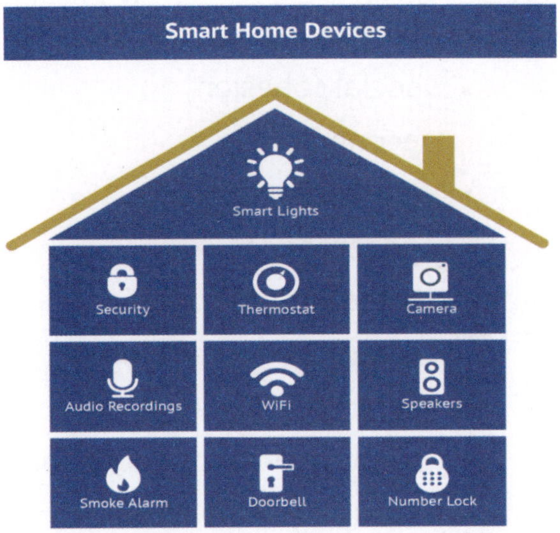

Future of Smart Homes

Home automation is changing the way of people for their daily tasks.

With the advancement in technology and increased access to technology, smart homes will be a very common sight in the coming days. AI is playing its role in home security, smart lighting or temperature control and making home life comfortable.

Boring tasks that take good time of people's lives will become completely automated. By doing so, Artificial Intelligence is making the goal of home automation a reality and reducing human involvement.

SMART CITY

The concept of a smart city lies in the use of technology to facilitate new experiences for its residents and users, to make living more comfortable and secure. The definition of a smart city varies from city to city and country to country, depending on the requirements of the residents of that city.

The top ten smart cities in the world are considered:

- London
- New York
- Amsterdam
- Paris
- Reykjavik
- Tokyo
- Singapore (Capital of the Republic of Singapore)
- Copenhagen
- Berlin
- Vienna.

These cities have been analysed on the basis of nine key points such as:

- human capital
- social cohesion
- economy
- environment
- governance
- urban planning
- international outreach
- technology
- mobility and transportation

Smart city features include:

- smart urban planning
- smart housings
- reducing traffic congestion
- reducing air pollution
- preserving and developing open spaces such as parks, playgrounds and recreational spaces
- promoting a variety of transport options
- making citizen-friendly location
- providing adequate infrastructure and more.

AI in a Smart City

AI and machine learning combined with the IoT (Internet of Things) can address many key challenges like:

- urban population
- water management
- energy crisis
- traffic management
- healthcare and businesses

What AI can Do for a Smart City?

- Smart water management: Technology helps us get our basic amenities like water, food, shelter, etc., and minimise the cost of living in cities.
- With AI, it is possible to:
- streamline the use of water
- streamline the use of power in a city.

Smart Grid Technology

It can be used to manage:

- the efficient use of power meters.

- the efficient use of water meters to locate leaks and prevent excess use of water.
- Smart lighting: Everybody wants streets to be properly lit. Streetlights are necessary and consume a lot of energy.
  - Use of smart lighting can reduce consumption of energy by allowing lighting only those areas when there is a need.
  - Lamps can be used to adjust the brightness based on the presence of pedestrians, cyclists or cars.
  - Lamp posts with additional sensors can be employed for security applications or serve as Wi-Fi network hotspots.
- **Smart Traffic Management:** AI-based smart traffic solutions can be used to ensure people moving from one point to another as safely and efficiently as possible. Sensors and CCTV cameras are installed on the roads to send real-time updates about traffic flow to a central traffic management system. Data feed from cameras are analysed and road-users are notified regarding congestion and traffic signal malfunctions.

- **Smart Parking:** Finding a parking slot especially during holiday time in cities becomes very difficult. Smart parking solutions can check whether parking slots are free or occupied. Smart parking creates a real-time parking map by using road sensors embedded in the ground of the parking area.

Smart City Features

(Indian Scenario, laid down by Smart Cities Mission, Ministry of Housing and Urban Affairs, GoI)

Some typical features of comprehensive development in Smart Cities are described below.

- Promoting mixed land use in area-based developments, planning for 'unplanned areas'. The States will enable some flexibility in land use and building bye-laws to adapt to change;
- Housing and inclusiveness expand housing opportunities for all;
- Creating walkable localities reduces congestion, air

Smart Cities in India (Round 1)

Bhubaneshwar	Indore
Pune	New Delhi
Jaipur	Coimbatore
Surat	Kakinada
Kochi	Belagavi
Ahmedabad	Udaipur
Jabalpur	Guwahati
Vishakhapatnam	Chennai
Solapur	Ludhiana
Devnagere	Bhopal

pollution and resource depletion, boost local economy, promote interactions and ensure security. The road network is created or refurbished not only for vehicles and public transport, but also for pedestrians and cyclists and necessary administrative services are offered within walking or cycling distance;

- Preserving and developing open spaces like parks, playgrounds and recreational spaces in order to enhance the quality of life of citizens, reduce the urban heat effects in areas and generally promote eco-balance;
- Promoting a variety of transport options— public transport and last mile para-transport connectivity;
- Making governance citizen-friendly and cost effective increasingly rely on online services to bring about accountability and transparency. Forming e-groups to listen to people and obtain feedback and use online monitoring of programs and activities with the aid of cyber tour of worksites; giving an identity to the city based on its main economic activity, such as local cuisine, health, education, arts and craft, culture, sports goods, furniture, hosiery, textile, dairy, etc;
- Applying Smart Solutions to infrastructure and services in area-based development in order to make them better.

  For Example:

  Making areas less vulnerable to disasters, using fewer resources and providing cheaper services.

- **Smart Waste Management:** Waste management is an essential city service. With the ever-increasing urban population, there is a need to adopt smart methods for waste management. Smart sensors fitted on waste bins can send notifications to authorities to dispatch waste collection trucks as soon as they are about to be full.
- Separate bins for paper, plastic, glass and waste food items should be maintained.
- Waste materials can be recycled and put to some other use.
- **Smart Police System:** Smart police system involves law enforcement agencies to employ evidence-based and data-driven strategies to have an effectively control in the city.

  For Example:

  A network of cameras and sensors can be installed in every corner to help identify people who commit crime, smoke in prohibited zones or look suspicious. Cameras can be used to monitor crowd density and vehicle movement in a particular area.

- **Smart Governance:** Smart governance implies the use of information and communication technology intelligently to reduce corruption in governments and public administration organisations.

The main goal is to improve decision-making in government and citizens. Smart governance uses data, evidence and other resources to improve decision-making.

ACTIVITY

SMART BUILDING

WHAT IS A SMART BUILDING?

A smart building is the one that uses advanced and integrated building technology systems. These systems include:

- building automation
- life safety
- telecommunications
- user systems
- facility management systems
- HVAC control. (HVAC stands for Heating, Ventilation and Air Conditioning control).

Smart buildings use Internet of Things (IoT) devices. These are; sensors, software and online connectivity. These devices monitor various building characteristics, analyze the data and generate insights around usage patterns and trends that can be used to optimize the building's environment and operations.

Smart building technology has many applications within a building, depending on your requirements and goals. Making a building smart starts with linking of core systems such as lighting, power meters, water meters, pumps, heating, fire alarms and chiller plants with sensors and control systems. At a more advanced stage elevators, access systems and shading can also be integrated with the system.

These benefits range from energy savings, productivity gains to sustainability. Smart building implementation can:

- reduce energy costs
- increase the productivity of the facility staff
- improve building operations
- support sustainability efforts
- enhance decision-making across the organization.

One example of energy efficiency is the use of optimal start/stop of AC unit, which allows the building automation system to learn when it should start the air conditioning system for a particular zone in the building. Another feature is electrical loads that are grouped into critical, high priority and non-essential categories.

HUMAN-MACHINE INTERACTION (HMI)

Human–machine interaction (HMI) means the communication and interaction between a human and a machine through a user interface. The machine is made to learn and learn. Machine learning is an important branch of artificial intelligence.

HMI is a component of certain devices that are capable of handling human-machine interactions. The goal of HMI development is to make computers serve human and and adapt to his needs.

Obtaining data from HMI enables us to learn more effectively and build smarter systems.

How does Human-Machine Interaction Work?

Smooth communication between people and machines requires an interface and a place where a user engages with the machine.

A computer machine can also be controlled by:

- text being keyed in
- a mouse
- touch screens
- voice or gestures

The devices are either controlled:

- directly by the users touching the smartphone's screen
- or by issue a verbal command
- or the system automatically identifies what people want.

There are also digital assistants like chatbots that reply automatically to the requests of customers and keep on learning.

One simple example is a light switch – the interface between the machine-light and a human being. It is also possible to differentiate between direct control, such as tapping a touch screen and automatic control. In automatic control, the system itself identifies what people want.

- Voice interaction based on machine learning
- Face recognition based on neural networks
- Gesture and motion recognition
- Smart medical analysis
- Computer-aided detection and diagnosis
- Brain-computer interface
- Analysis of human factors in the design of machines
- Deep learning models for medical image reconstruction, restoration and registration.

EXERCISE

Performance Assessment, Review and Analysis

Fill in the Blanks with Given Hints

1. ______________ uses Artificial Intelligence for filtering spams.
2. Plagiarism means ______________ Some else's work.
3. A computer is trained to see the images. It is using______________ .
4. ______________ is AI powered personal assistant.
5. Smart home reduces or eliminates ______________efforts.

HINTS

Computer Vision, Alexa, copying, human, Email

Write T for True and F for False

1. Car riding taxi services use machine learning in their system. [ ]
2. Self-driven car uses AI. [ ]
3. Neural network is a subset of Artificial Intelligence. [ ]
4. Google Doc can be used as Story Speaker. [ ]
5. DeepText in Facebook uses machine learning for image recognition. [ ]

Multiple Choice Questions

Tick [✓] the best alternatives.

1. *Smart reply* of Google is useful in which area?

   (a) Alexa devices [ ] (b) Email checking [ ]

   (c) Online shopping [ ] (d) None of these [ ]

2. Robo-Readers are used for ______________.
   (a) Online ordering [ ] (b) Banking applications [ ]
   (c) Grading [ ] (d) Power control [ ]
3. AI in smart home can be helpful in ______________.
   (a) Door surveillance [ ] (b) Motion sensoring [ ]
   (c) AC control [ ] (d) All of these [ ]
4. Which of the following applications can be used for story writing?
   (a) MS-Word [ ] (b) Google Chrome [ ]
   (c) Google Smart Reply [ ] (d) Google Doc [ ]
5. Which of the following is Google's messaging service using AI?
   (a) Facebook [ ] (b) WhatsApp [ ]
   (c) Bingo [ ] (d) Allo [ ]
6. A smart home can ______________.
   (a) save energy [ ] (b) monitor surveillance [ ]
   (c) help disabled persons [ ] (d) All of these [ ]
7. Which of the following aspects is not covered under Smart City?
   (a) Safety [ ] (b) Traffic management [ ]
   (c) Grooming [ ] (d) Environment [ ]
8. Which of the following is a product of Google?
   (a) Siri [ ] (b) Alexa [ ]
   (c) Watson [ ] (d) None of these [ ]
9. Which of the following is the major requirement for Smart Homes?
   (a) Local Area Network (LAN) [ ] (b) Bluetooth [ ]
   (c) WiFi [ ] (d) Internet Connectivity [ ]
10. In HVAC, 'A' stands for ______________ .
   (a) Artificial [ ] (b) Analysis [ ]
   (c) Air [ ] (d) Accurate [ ]

Activity Based Questions

STORY SPEAKER

Story Speaker lets anyone create talking, interactive stories with no coding required. Just write your story in a Google Doc, push a button and every Google Home device linked to your account can play it, instantly.

When you start Google Doc, you are asked to sign in with Google account (Gmail account also works).

After successful authentication, Google Doc opens on the screen.

You can write your story in Google Doc.

Story Speaker lets anyone create talking, interactive stories with no coding required. Just write your story in a Google Doc, push a button and every Google Home device linked to your account can play it.

If you are typing your story on Smart Home, you may take the following points into consideration for your dream AI-powered Smart Home:

- Surveillance
- Motion Sensor
- Door Control
- Security and Alarm
- Environment monitoring
- Energy management
- Light control
- Fan speed control
- Temperature monitoring (Thermostat)
- AC control
- Remote control
- Internet gateway
- Set-top box
- Window control

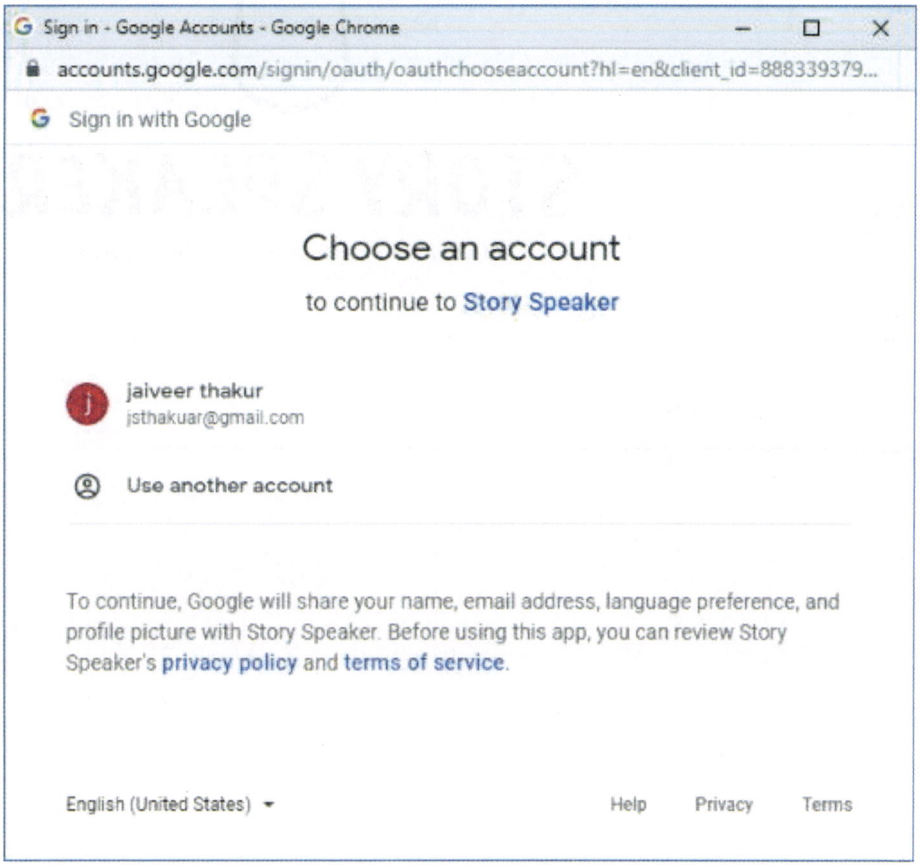

When you type a story in Google Doc, you have to save its copy by clicking File > Make a copy. Give suitable name to your story file.

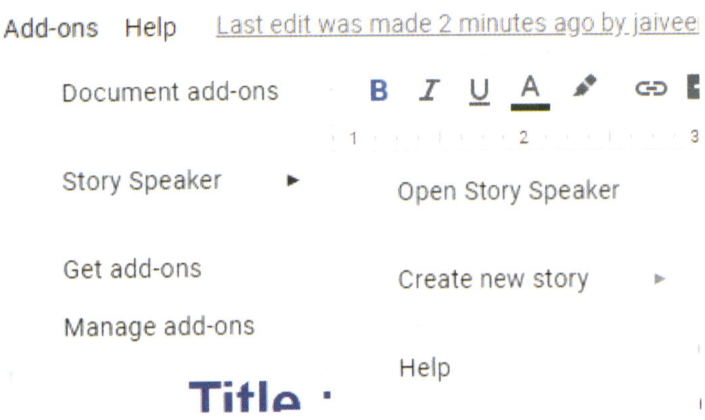

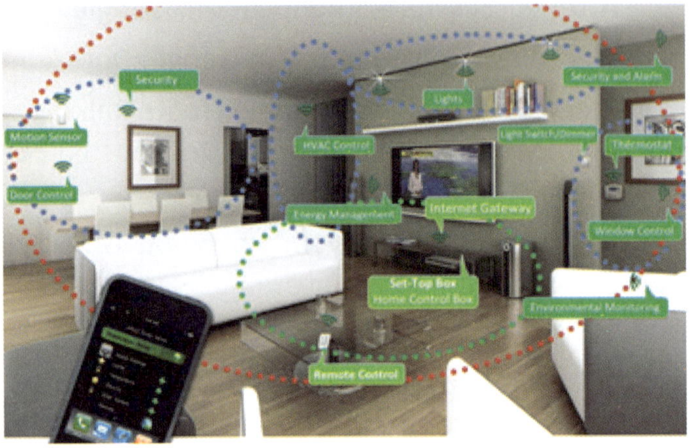

You can also create a new story, by clicking Add-ons > Story Speaker > Create new story > From basic template or From advanced template.

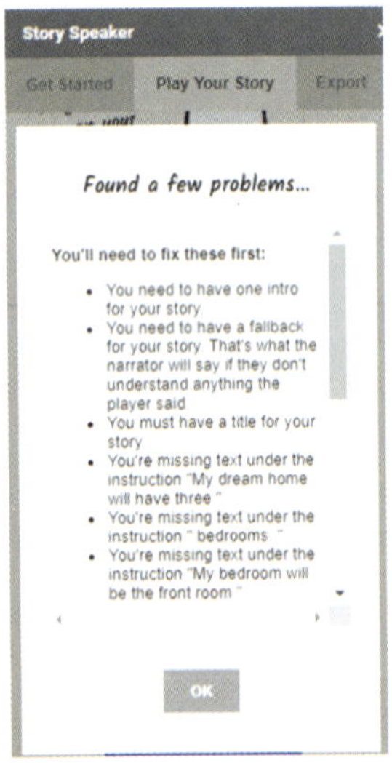

To start a story speaker, click Add-ons > Story Speaker > Open Story Speaker.

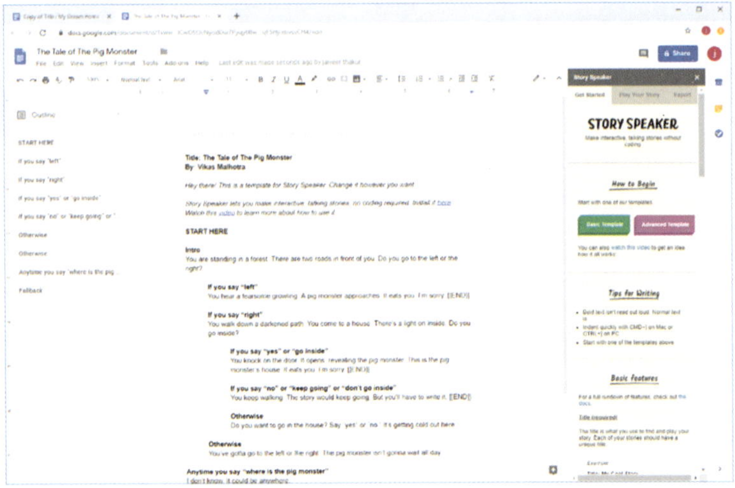

When you try to play story, Story Speaker checks for errors.

If everything is okay, your story is played.

You do not need to know how to code. Basic and advanced templates get you writing quickly.

There is a lot Story Speaker can do, including respond to what players say, give random responses and remember what the player said.

You can even export your story and so anyone with a Google Home can hear it.

Useful links:

https://workspace.google.com/marketplace/app/story_speaker/888339379807

Scan the code

https://experiments.withgoogle.com/collection/ai

Scan the code

Competency Based Question

1. Which of the following applications of AI are your aware of?

   Select: I know about it - if you have knowledge or seen it.

   Select: I can imagine it – if you have only read or heard about it.

   Select: I do not know – if you have not heard or imagine about it.

   Tick (✓) the appropriate balloon.

Smart House	I know about it / I can imagine it / I do not know	Smart City	I know about it / I can imagine it / I do not know
Digital Assistants	I know about it / I can imagine it / I do not know	Smart Building	I know about it / I can imagine it / I do not know
Customer Service	I know about it / I can imagine it / I do not know	Banking Service	I know about it / I can imagine it / I do not know

Cyber Security	I know about it · I can imagine it · I do not know	Online Recommendations	I know about it · I can imagine it · I do not know
Fraud Detection	I know about it · I can imagine it · I do not know	Weather Forecast	I know about it · I can imagine it · I do not know
Criminal Detection	I know about it · I can imagine it · I do not know	Airflight Movements	I know about it · I can imagine it · I do not know
Traffic Management	I know about it · I can imagine it · I do not know	Agriculture	I know about it · I can imagine it · I do not know
Operation Theater	I know about it · I can imagine it · I do not know	Medical Care	I know about it · I can imagine it · I do not know

Answer the Following Questions

1. What are the uses of AI in daily activities?

___

___

2. How can be AI useful in schools? Write any three areas.

___

___

3. How is it possible to recognize faces for a system?

___

___

4. Write any five things you would like to have in your AI-powered house.

___

___

5. Write the names of AI-powered technologies you are using in your daily life.

____

____

6. What are the features of a smart city?

____

____

LAB ACTIVITY

For Students

- Make a presentation on Artificial Intelligence showing the applications of AI in the following areas:
- Schools
- Smart Homes

Discuss:

- How machines are able to give results on the basis of input?
- Artificial Intelligence in Social Networking.

For Teachers

- Explore the use of Story Speaker and creating a story through Google Doc and ask the students to write their own imaginations for creating their home as Smart Home using AI.

  Moreover, the concept of Smart City is also emerging. You may put questions to the students what would they want or do for their city to be a smart city.

3

PURPOSE

Introduction

The Sustainable Development Goals (SDGs) also known as the Global Goals, were adopted by all United Nations Member States in 2015 as a universal call to action to end poverty, protect the planet and ensure that all people enjoy peace and prosperity by 2030. The number of goals is 17.

Our track record of working on the goals provides us a valuable experience and can help us reach the targets set out in the SDGs by 2030. But we cannot do this alone.

Achieving the SDGs requires the partnership of governments, private sector, civil society and citizens alike to make sure we leave a better planet for future generations. AI enables new technologies that improve efficiency and productivity and can be very helpful in achieving the SDGs.

Learning Outcomes

- To understand the impact of Artificial Intelligence on Sustainable Development Goals to develop responsible citizenship.

Coverage:

Introduction to sustainable development goals.

INTRODUCTION TO SUSTAINABLE DEVELOPMENT (SD)

To understand the use of AI in Sustainable Development, we have to first understand the theoretical concepts of SD.

Sustainable development is in the news almost every day as the world copes with climate change, biodiversity loss and conflict and scarcity of resources.

"Sustainable development is development that meets the needs of the present without compromising the ability of future generations to meet their own needs."

World Commission on Environment and Development

Economists have also provided a definition of sustainable development as being an economic process in which the quantity and quality of our stocks of natural resources (like forests) and the integrity of biogeochemical cycles (like climate) are sustained and passed on to the future generations unimpaired.

In other words, there is no depreciation in the world's "natural capital".

Sustainable development ties together the concerns for natural resources with the economic, social and political challenges being faced by the humanity.

It is the responsibility of present generation to use natural resources wisely and regenerate, maintain and improve natural resources for survival and existence of future generations.

Examples of Sustainable Development

- **Solar Energy:** The most significant advantage of solar energy is that it is completely free and is available in limitless supply. Both of these factors provide a huge benefit to consumers and reduce pollution. Replacing non-renewable energy with this type of energy is effective both environmentally and financially.
- **Wind Energy:** Wind energy is another readily available source of energy. Harnessing the power of wind energy requires the use of windmills. Wind energy can supplement or even replace the cost of grid power and therefore, it is a good investment and a great example of sustainable development.
- **Crop Rotation:** Crop rotation is defined as the successive planting of different crops on the same land to improve soil fertility and control insects and crop diseases.

  This farming practice is beneficial in several ways, because it is chemical-free. Crop rotation has been proven to maximize the growth potential of land and it also prevents disease and insects in the soil.
- **Efficient Water Fixtures:** Replacing current construction practices and supporting the installation of efficient shower heads, toilets and other water appliances can conserve water.
- **Green Space:** Green spaces include parks and other areas where plants and wildlife are encouraged to thrive.

  Advantages of green spaces include:
  - Regulating air quality and climate.
  - Reducing energy consumption.
  - Recharging groundwater supplies.

IMPORTANCE OF SUSTAINABLE DEVELOPMENT

The major goal of sustainable development is to meet the needs of today, without compromising the needs of tomorrow.

We cannot continue using current levels of resources at the current pace, as this will not leave enough for future generations.

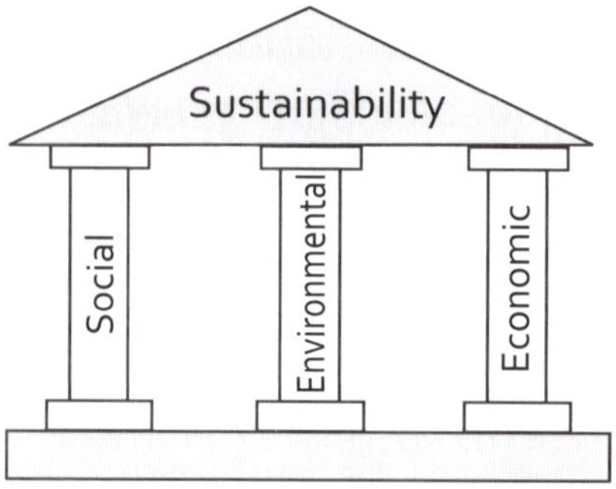

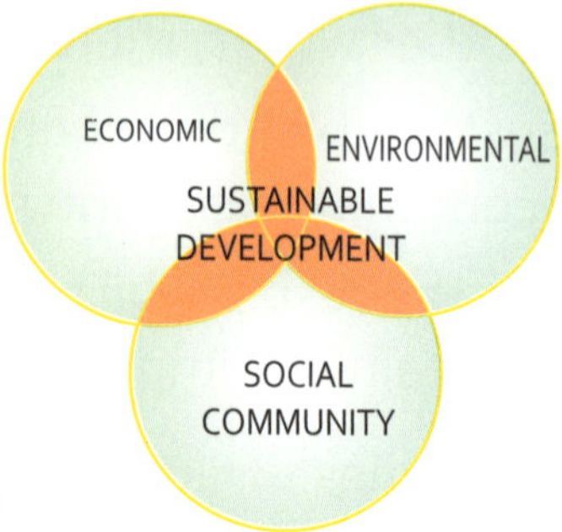

Stabilizing and reducing carbon emissions is a major key to living within environmental limits.

There are three major components of sustainable developments:

- Social Growth
- Environmental Growth
- Economic Growth

All these three components are correlated with well being of individuals and society.

Importance of Sustainable Development can be seen upon through the following points:

- Sustainability is the concept that recognizes the natural systems which are essential to provide both economic needs and quality of life.
- Sustainable Development connects whole space and time. It is not limited only to one community.
- It needs cooperation of people from different societies and geographies.
- It is a continuous process.
- SD contributes to growth, profit and development.
- It helps in developing eco-friendly global culture.
- It concerns for limited capacity of natural resources with social challenges facing humanity.
- It aims at protecting and managing natural resources for economic and social development.
- It considers the needs of future generation.
- It aims at achieving the goal of economic and social development without destroying the earth's natural resources. It focuses on conserving natural resources for future generation.

Sustainable Development Goals

In 2015, 195 nations agreed with the United Nation that they can change the world for the better.

This will be accomplished by bringing together their respective governments, businesses, media, institutions of higher education and local NGOs to improve the lives of the people in their country by the year 2030.

On 1 January 2016, the 17 Sustainable Development Goals (SDGs) of the 2030 Agenda for Sustainable Development (which were adopted by world leaders in September 2015 at an historic UN Summit) came into force.

All the 17 goals of the Sustainable Development have been shown in the icon forms as given in the above picture.

These 17 goals are as follows:

Goal 1. End poverty in all its forms everywhere.

Goal 2. End hunger, achieve food security and improved nutrition and promote sustainable agriculture

Goal 3. Ensure healthy lives and promote well-being for all at all ages

Goal 4. Ensure inclusive and equitable quality education and promote lifelong learning opportunities for all

Goal 5. Achieve gender equality and empower all women and girls

Goal 6. Ensure availability and sustainable management of water and sanitation for all

Goal 7. Ensure access to affordable, reliable, sustainable and modern energy for all

Goal 8. Promote sustained, inclusive and sustainable economic growth, full and productive employment and decent work for all

Goal 9. Build resilient infrastructure, promote inclusive and sustainable industrialization and foster innovation

Goal 10. Reduce inequality within and among countries

Goal 11. Make cities and human settlements inclusive, safe, resilient and sustainable

Goal 12. Ensure sustainable consumption and production patterns

Goal 13. Take urgent action to combat climate change and its impacts

Goal 14. Conserve and sustainably use the oceans, seas and marine resources for sustainable development

Goal 15. Protect, restore and promote sustainable use of terrestrial ecosystems, sustainably manage forests, combat desertification and halt and reverse land degradation and halt biodiversity loss

Goal 16. Promote peaceful and inclusive societies for sustainable development, provide access to justice for all and build effective, accountable and inclusive institutions at all level

Goal 17. Strengthen the means of implementation and revitalize the global partnership for sustainable development.

APPLICATIONS OF AI IN SUSTAINABLE DEVELOPMENT

Below are some examples of areas of application for sustainable development.

No Poverty

AI can expand the socio-economic benefits of existing technologies. It can lead different alternatives to reach remote areas that lack education, social assistance and productive capacities. AI can be a decisive instrument to remove poverty.

AI can help to identify regions that need help the most. It can tackle poverty in particular areas by:

- improving farming and agriculture
- increasing education
- helping citizens learn new skills to support communities.

Zero Hunger

Using AI technologies, effectiveness of food supply chains can improve efficiency and reduce wastage.

AI can provide support for farmers' decision making and increase in productivity.

Roughly one third of all food is wasted, representing 8% of global greenhouse gas emissions. AI can be deployed across the food and agriculture chain to:

- check food waste
- reduce crop loss at the farm level
- improve storage, distribution and processing of fresh food
- to reduce food waste

Good Health and Well Being

AI is being used to improve the ability of healthcare professionals to diagnose and treat diseases such as cancer and glaucoma. Many of these cases use machine learning to diagnose disease, *e.g.*, Google's work on detecting lung cancer.

AI brings efficiency and allows doctors to spend more time on higher value activities. AI can be particularly beneficial in regions that lack health care professionals for medical tasks. Machines might perform such tasks like reading CT scans.

AI is increasingly being used to optimize the allocation of basic health services and the organization of administrative tasks.

For Example:

AI planning can improve the scheduling of health visitors, while natural language processing can be used to simplify clinical documentation and enable voice-to-text dictation.

Through AI, it is possible to monitor patient populations and medical data to predict outbreaks of infectious diseases and public health emergencies. Through modelling cause-and-effect relationships, this can allow public health agencies to investigate and mitigate in real-time the progression of epidemics. In the Covid-19 pandemic, AI has been extensively used in various countries.

Quality Education

Improve learning outcomes through analysis of data.

Gender Equality

AI-powered gender-decoders help employers. They can use gender-sensitive language to write job postings that are more effective in order to increase the diversity of their workforce. AI has the potential to provide the solution for advancing gender equality in the societies.

Clean Water and Sanitation

AI has the potential to resolve challenges related to clean water and sanitation. It helps municipalities to manage their water and wastewater systems to ensure a clean and sanitized water supply.

An IoT device (sensor) can classify and detect dangerous bacteria and harmful particles. The system can run continuously in real time. The cities can install IoT devices (sensors) across different water sources to monitor water quality as well as contamination in real time. These sensors have Internet connectivity.

> **Note**
> IoT stands for Internet of Things.

Affordable and Clean Energy

Optimise energy generation and reduce environmental impact through analysis of operational and environmental data.

Help consumers to find the most affordable and clean energy resources by using AI agents.

Decent Work and Economic Growth

"Despite legitimate concerns about automation replacing jobs, AI augmentation and targeted automation with intelligent devices can improve the work environment, increase productivity and be a significant driver of economic growth." — AI XPRIZE

AI technologies are being used to reduce need for human work on dangerous work such as mining, repetitive factory and agricultural work and dangerous industrial work.

AI can be used in evaluating and appraising business loan applications, using past successes and failures as training data to judge benefits of new loans.

There are several job platforms that are using AI for screening, interviewing and recommending the job-seekers to the recruiters.

AngelList, LinkedIn, Meetup, Jobcase etc are scanning the resumes of the job-seekers using AI-powered programs.

Industry, Innovation and Infrastructure

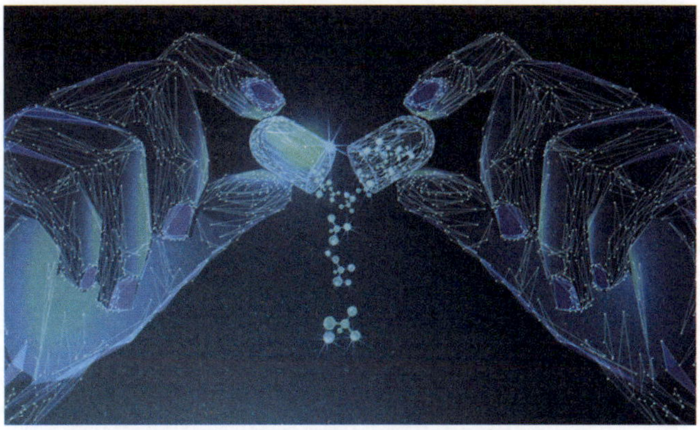

AI can assist decision making in innovation management. There are many applications of AI systems in materials discovery. AI can be used to optimize battery components and solar cells. For this, machine learning-based methods are used to predict the most promising materials to test, thereby speeding up the innovation process.

In pharmaceutical research and development, AI systems include uses that speed up the process of protein engineering, which is helpful in discovering proteins suitable for technological, scientific and medical applications.

There are many ways that the infrastructure industry can apply computer vision or AI in general. It can use reality modelling applications and their ability to classify images. By creating 3D models, users will have better visibility into their project's progress and end-goals. It accelerates the design process.

Reduced Inequalities

AI-based technologies are taking into account the needs of people with disabilities and improve their living conditions.

Microsoft's Seeing AI and Google's Lookout applications help blind or visually impaired people to identify elements (individuals, objects, text, etc.) present in their surroundings using automatic image recognition.

The idea is to put AI at the service of equal opportunity. It should be able to fight against discriminations at the workplace.

Several things are going in this direction, *e.g.*, the tools aiming to limit bias during recruitment.

Textio is a smart text editor which is capable of making a job description in a better way. Using this editor, the software publisher Atlassian took the percentage of women recruited from 10 to 57%.

In France, the Data for Good community unites hundreds of voluntary data scientists, developers and designers, who put their skills in projects of social impact.

Sustainable Cities and Communities

The use of artificial intelligence in smart cities can be life changing if implemented in the proper places. There are multiple zones in cities where AI can be used to improve the performance and efficiency of an Urban Development system.

AI-enabled cameras and sensors can keep an eye on the surroundings to enhance security level in the city's neighbourhoods.

Sensors are used for vehicle parking and traffic management system.

Responsible Consumption and Production

- AI brings efficiency in global food supply chains
- It enables better forecasting of consumer and retailer demands through historical and real-time data (which ultimately means less food waste).
- AI is being deployed with other digital technology to enable more efficient food production (*i.e.*, more food with fewer inputs).
- AI helps farmers to better know the weather patterns and adjust planting based on supply and demand. It helps them in fighting pests and optimizing inputs(water, fertilizer, pesticides, etc.)
- AI is being deployed in the development of more sustainable products, *e.g.*, alternative protein-manufacturing are using AI to identify the right combination of ingredients that mimic animal products.

Climate Action

AI powered solutions allow swift, dependable and rigorous baselining of the entire emission footprint, with improved accuracy, AI based forecasts and simulations.

Google's "Hydronet" is an example. This can play a role in accurately detecting vital weak spots to prepare for extreme river floods. The solution was adopted for helping in improving flood forecasting in India and Bangladesh. It had covered over 250 million people who were exposed to the risk.

Life in Water

New AI innovations are beginning to enhance the protection of fisheries, the identification of pollution hotspots and giving early warnings of natural disasters.

AI can also measure and assess water quality.

Microscopic plankton species are key indicators for ocean pollution levels, since small changes in their health can point to much larger water quality issues. They are also the base of the ocean food chain.

IBM is developing microscopes that assess the health of plankton in their natural environment, while aggregating data on a cloud-based network.

They are also exploring for such technology to provide early detection for oil spills and red tides and toxicity in the water. AI has made it possible to monitor the health of the ocean in real-time, allowing for more timely preventive action.

Ocean is a major source for lives but it can also be a dangerous and destructive force. Climate changes are expected to increase the frequency and severity of extreme ocean events.

AI sensors are being tested by Liquid Ocean(a part of the Boeing Company) to provide early warnings of hurricanes from ocean indicators.

Other ventures are exploring the use of AI to assess the damage of climate change.

The ocean has long been a challenge for scientists. Developments in AI for the ocean may help them in scanning the oceans planning as how to protect ourselves and life below water from environmental threats.

Life on Land

AI technology can play an important role in environmental protection. The management of protected areas can be made more effective with a clear understanding of the specific behaviour patterns.

AI can in the future be applied to thousands of issues affecting the environment.

For Example:

Using AI and data from NASA, researchers are able to identify patterns and monitor changes of land surfaces, such as decreasing sea area, decreasing ice caps surface area.

Peace, Justice and Strong Institutions

AI could have a positive impact on 58% of the targets in the SDG (SDG-16) "Peace, Justice and strong institutions". If deployed ethically, AI can contribute to justice systems by:

- improving accessibility
- facilitating communication
- assisting administration.

Partnerships for the Goals

Access to the internet and innovative services enabled by mobile connectivity are contributing to the fulfilment of all the SDGs.

Scaling IoT and other emerging technologies, which will require collaboration and investment from both the private and public sectors.

AI can help to reach the SDGs		
2 ZERO HUNGER	3 GOOD HEALTH AND WELL-BEING	4 QUALITY EDUCATION
Computer vision based on satellite, drone or even phone images can help farmers protect their crops and increase their yields by detecting plant damage early and getting recommendations on fertilizing, watering and harvesting.	Machine learning can help to map and predict outbreaks of diseases and wildfires based on satellite images and other data, so governments and organizations can prepare and react quicker.	Natural Language Processing can help increase the quality and inclusiveness of education, by giving students automated feedback on exercises and adapting their level of difficulty.
10 REDUCED INEQUALITIES	13 CLIMATE ACTION	14 LIFE BELOW WATER
Image recognition and speech processing can enable easier identification of individuals and thus easier access to financial, health and education services.	IoT networks of small microphones combined with speech processing can detect chain-saw sounds in forests to detect and locate illegal activities. *(IoT means Internet of Things)*	Computer vision based on satellite images can track illegal fishing activities, so they can be stopped and fishing populations can recover.

EXERCISE

Performance Assessment, Review and Analysis

Fill in the Blanks with Given Hints

1. The number one goal of SDG is ______________.
2. There are ______________ pillars of sustainability.
3. ______________ can help in improving quality of education.
4. NLP is a branch of ______________.
5. ______________ can help in predicting outbreak of diseases.

HINTS

Three, NLP, AI, ML, No Poverty

Write T for True and F for False

1. NLP stands for Neutral Language Processing. [ ]
2. ML stands for Manual Learning. [ ]
3. AI is a branch of NLP. [ ]
4. CV stands for Computer Vision. [ ]
5. CV is used for image processing and recognition. [ ]

Multiple Choice Questions

Tick [✓] the best alternatives.

1. Which of the following is a branch of AI?
   (a) Machine Learning [ ] (b) Computer Vision [ ]
   (c) Natural Language Processing [ ] (d) All of these [ ]

2. For speech recognition and help in education, _______________ is helpful.

(a) NLP [ ] (b) ML [ ]

(c) CV [ ] (d) None of these [ ]

3. The number of goals in SDG is _______________.

(a) 7 [ ] (b) 17 [ ]

(c) 27 [ ] (d) 37 [ ]

4. The target to achieve SDGs is by_______________.

(a) 2025 [ ] (b) 2030 [ ]

(c) 2032 [ ] (d) 2035 [ ]

5. Which of the following is an icon for Climate Action?

(a)  [ ] (b)  [ ]

(c)  [ ] (d)  [ ]

6. In which year, the SDGs were adopted by the world leaders?

(a) 2010 [ ] (b) 2012 [ ]

(c) 2015 [ ] (d) 2017 [ ]

7. On which date, the SDGs officially came into force?

(a) January 1, 2015 [ ] (b) January 1, 2016 [ ]

(c) January 1, 2017 [ ] (d) January 1, 2018 [ ]

8. Globally there is a much talk about Artificial Intelligence and its adoption in achievement of Sustainable Development Goals, but yet there is a dearth of skills in Artificial Intelligence and its adoption. What is the reason for that?

(a) Lack of funds availability from governments [ ]

(b) Lack of support for adoption of AI technologies [ ]

(c) Inadequate development in the field of AI [ ]

(d) Lack of quality and freely available data [ ]

9. Read the given statements and select the correct answer from the given options.

Statement 1. Recycling and reuse of waste products and materials is one of the measures of sustainable development.

Statement 2. Recycling involves only scientific management of waste products and material.

(a) Both the statements are true

(b) Both the statements are false

(c) Statement 1 is true but Statement 2 is false

(d) Statement 1 is false but Statement 2 is true

Activity Based Questions

SUSTAINABLE DEVELOPMENT GOALS

Our aim is to help people understand their role in the future of the planet as individuals, team players and most importantly, as responsible global citizens. In order to build a better world for everyone and the planet, the Member States of the United Nations have agreed to do their utmost to achieve 17 Sustainable Development Goals (SDGs) by 2030. We need younger generations to be key players for a brighter future. For this purpose, we have created the "Go Goals!" game for children aged 8-10. Designed to be fun and engaging, this game informs children while motivating them to actively pursue the SDGs. Your role as an educator is crucial! With help from people like you, your family, your friends and community, we will be able to achieve the goals. Remember: even small steps can help to make a big difference if millions around the world are involved! We hope that you enjoy this game! You are invited to download it and follow the instructions and rules below. Thank you for making the world a better place!

SUSTAINABLE DEVELOPMENT GOALS

HOW TO PLAY THE GAME

There are 63 spaces on the board game. Players advance the number of spaces determined by rolling a single dice.

Each player places their token on the Start field.

Players take turns to roll the dice and move their tokens forward the number of spaces as shown on the dice

- If a player lands at the bottom of a ladder, they can immediately climb to the top
- If a player lands at the top of a waterslide, they immediately move to the bottom of the slide
- If a player lands on a Sustainable Development Goal field (1-17), they can draw a card corresponding to the goal number. Another player should read the card question. A correct answer from the card drawer will allow the player to roll the dice once again

The first player to arrive on the field '2030' is the winner! If a player throws the required number, they must step forward into field '2030' and then move backwards the surplus number of spaces

HOW TO CONTRIBUTE TO THE SDGs

Change begins with us. We need to make sure we are well informed about the causes and possible solutions to the world's issues. Only then can we make small positive actions in our everyday lives: from talking constructively with our families, friends and communities, to organizing ourselves and urging governments to listen to the voices of their citizens.

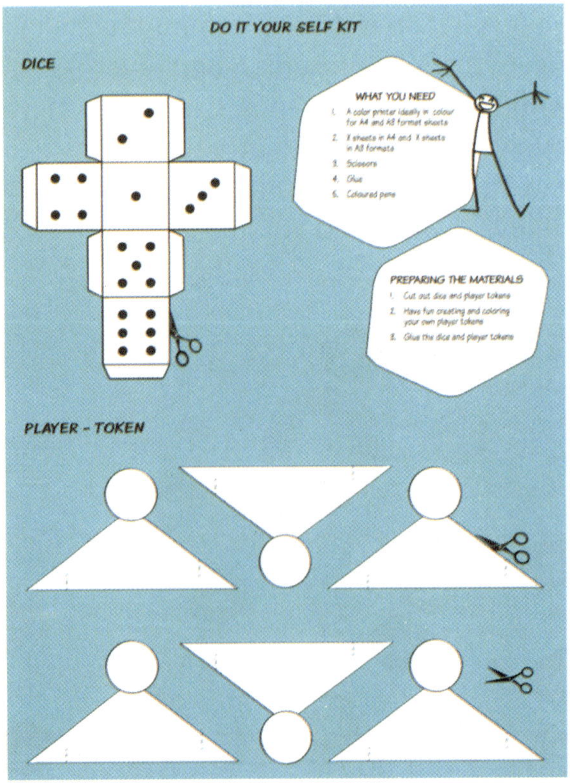

Sample Quiz

Some sample questions on SDGs have been given below:

Competency Based Questions

1. There are 17 sustainable development goals and below are the 17 pictures of which each one is associated with the SDG. Write the name of SDG below the picture.

 1	 2	 3	 4
 5	 6	 7	 8
 9	 10	 11	 12
 13	 14	 15	 16
 17			

2. In the above 17 pictures, you have used your skills to mention the appropriate SDG.

   Now, in the following series of questions, we are giving you the exact pictures as used by the UNO for SDGs. You have to carefully observe each picture and write the SD Goal number for it

3. You have read in the chapter that there are three components of sustainable development; Social, Environmental, Economic.

   All the 17 SDGs can be classified under these three components.

   For Example:

   Goal 1, *i.e.,* End Poverty or No Poverty falls under Society Component.

   On the basis of components, you have to mention the Goal-number in the given balloons against given again each component.

Social	1										
Environmental											
Economic											

4. You have now enough read and knowledge about 17 SDGs. Out of these SDGs, a few ones are as such you can contribute individually.

   For Example:

   You can contribute to combat climate change by lowering carbon emissions or other harmful gases. This is the SD Goal number 13. But you cannot contribute to combat for the life below water (for sea-living beings), *i.e.* SD Goal number 14.

Now, you have to tick the choice you think the action you can take individually.

1. No Poverty	I can contribute	Cannot Contribute
2. Zero Hunger	I can contribute	Cannot Contribute
3. Gender Equality	I can contribute	Cannot Contribute
4. Quality Education	I can contribute	Cannot Contribute
5. Responsible Consumption	I can contribute	Cannot Contribute
6. Climate Action	I can contribute	Cannot Contribute
7. Affordable Energy	I can contribute	Cannot Contribute

Answer the Following Questions

1. What is the meaning of SDG?

____

____

2. Write any four goals of SDG.

____

____

3. Write any three SD goals which are related with social growth.

____

____

4. How is AI helpful in Quality Education? Mention the activities keeping in view your own school.

____

____

5. What is the role of NLP in AI?

____

____

6. How machine learning is helpful in the field of medicines and health services?

____

____

7. Write the area of use of Computer Vision.

____

____

LAB ACTIVITY

For Students

Make a presentation on SDG showing the applications of AI in achieving goals of SDG

Group Discussion:

Discuss in the group of 4 students:

- Use of NLP in SDGs.
- Use of CV.

For Teachers

- Sustainable Development Goals are the talks of all major conferences and meets in the world. You may discuss the need of achieving SDGs for achieving sustainability in the world. What contribution AI can give towards achieving the SDGs.

  You may explain the students the importance of SDGs with some examples.

4 POSSIBILITIES

Introduction

Artificial Intelligence has opened up numerous possibilities for the future.

From interpreting of audio and visual data to space exploration and moon-landing programs, AI is making waves across industries, making impossible things possible.

Almost every business need AI professionals to interpret business and market trends, clean raw data, build AI tools and use the AI boom to their advantage.

There has been a significant growth in AI careers and several possibilities and opportunities have been there for this field.

Learning Outcomes

- To research and develop awareness of skills required for jobs of the future.
- To imagine, examine and reflect on the skills required for the futuristic opportunities.
- To develop effective communication and collaborative work skills.

Coverage:

Futuristic job opportunities, Skills required for futuristic jobs, Career path in the field of Artificial Intelligence.

With more and more developments in the different branches of AI, be it Natural Language Processing, Computer Vision or any other branch of AI, the demand for AI-skilled people are increasing.

To cope up with the future challenges, one has to develop skills required for future jobs. Awareness is the first thing to be created among the future job seekers for preparing themselves for the AI environment.

Let us study about the job opportunities in the field of Artificial Intelligence.

FUTURISTIC JOB OPPORTUNITIES

New technologies are emerging and we are increasingly blending work and life for a new reality. We have never been more globally connected than we are today and a new set of jobs, skills and mindsets are emerging to succeed in an unpredictable future.

Analyst

Artificial intelligence and robotics will have a major impact on the future of work, putting business analysts in a great demand. These business forecasters can help companies make informed business decisions and they can play a big role in greater use of artificial intelligence.

Banking and Finance

In the present technological age, banking and finance professionals will be the innovators to lead businesses into the future. A good understanding of technology such as blockchain, crypto-currencies and digital reality will be required to lead the banking and finance world into the new age.

Communications

Automation, digital platforms and other innovations are changing the basic nature of work, putting greater emphasis on the importance of strong communication skills.

Knowledge-Intensive Jobs

Jobs of the future will be knowledge-intensive. Such knowledge-intensive roles give well-educated people the opportunity to contribute to their employer in a meaningful and effective way.

Networking (Communicating)

The ability to network(communicate) effectively will continue to be one of the most essential personal skills for business persons. Knowing how to communicate, inspire and unite ideas contributed by others can open doors in any industry you have to work in.

Robotics

Chat bots that foster human connections have made it into companies and are already allowing banks and large organisations to use technology to innovate and create greater efficiencies.

Artificial Intelligence *vs* Robotics

Artificial Intelligence is the intelligent use of Computer Science. It includes creating projects which would require human intelligence and exhibit artificial intelligence.

Man-made intelligence calculations can handle learning, critical thinking, language-understanding. Artificial Intelligence is utilized from smaller to advanced thinks like self-driving vehicle. Sometimes people represent AI as robots intently. Robotics is a part of innovation which manages robots. Robots are programmable machines which are normally ready to do a progression of activities self-sufficiently to some or full extent for which they are programmed.

There are three principle significant elements which comprise a robot:

- Robots cooperate with the actual world through sensors and actuators.
- Robots are programmable.
- Robots are normally self-ruling or semi-self-governing.

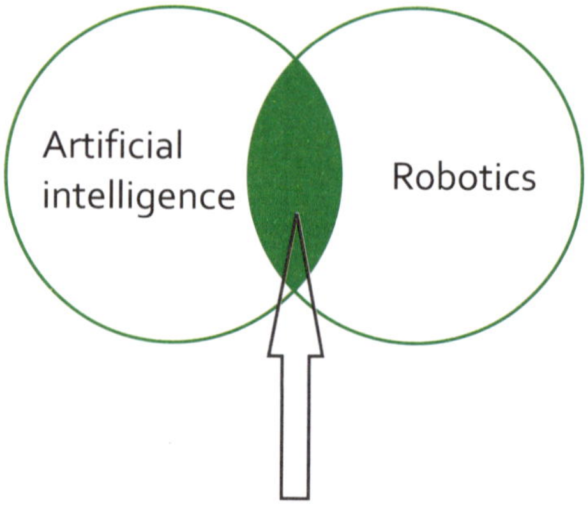

Robots are normally self-ruling because not all the robots are self-ruling.

Many robots are not artificially intelligent.

SKILLS REQUIRED FOR FUTURISTIC JOBS

It is not the thing that AI will continue to grow at its own. It would have to depend on human skills to stay and grow.

The following are the job skills of the future that Bots cannot master.

Creativity

There is no other thing which can overpower human imagination and creativity.

Having an imagination and thinking outside the box means that you can come up with ideas and that do not already exist.

While AI machines can create art, music and write. They do so by recognizing patterns and analysing data as opposed to producing something new.

Coming up with the initial ideas that have not previously existed is unique skill of human.

Ability to think and create new ideas solves the problems that machines cannot do. They do what they are taught.

For Example:

Suppose a person works in recruitment department. The goal of their office is to attract candidates to the company job page. The person will think new ways to attract applicants. They can experiment with various methods such as social media to find the best way to source applicants.

If a machine were in charge of sourcing candidates, it would only utilize channels which it has previously "learned" based on the data used.

Ability to Understand

Another thing that makes human superior than machines is the ability to understand others. This is highly useful in service-related fields dealing with people.

For Example:

An AI recruitment software can do the work in the initial stages of qualifying candidates by conducting interviews. But after that, to complete the hiring process, a human would need to be involved to physically meet candidates and make the final decision.

No matter how developed AI chatbots become, they will not have the ability to connect with and understand people on an emotional level to make final decisions. Bots cannot "see" inside of the other person and that is the special skill of human to interpret feelings, working style, effective communicating skills of others.

Planning

On the basis of coding and algorithm, it is easy for a computer to 'learn.'

For Example:

If you are playing tic-toe-tac game against a computer, you will know that is as competent and competitive as playing against a real person. Such games are bound by rules and the result is based on the logic.

A computer has already learnt the rules through coding.

For Example:

"if this, then that". On that rule-based coding, it is very quick for a computer to decide the rule.

But when it comes to real-world, the predictions are not as accurate for machines like playing games.

Many jobs require planning for uncertain outcomes, shifting priorities and filling information gaps. These skills are possessed only by human and not machines.

Judgement

A bot cannot replace a lawyer and judges in legal matters. In matters related to ethics, things are not always black and white.

In the position of a lawyer or a judge, both involve a higher level of thinking and decision making. This cannot be replaced by a bot.

Career Paths in Artificial Intelligence

The list below includes jobs in AI but also some positions that work closely with those in AI roles.

Career Path	Description/Job Role
Data Analytics	The role of the Data Analytics person is to find meaningful patterns in data by looking at the past to help make predictions about the future.

Researcher	The role of Researcher is related to Computer Science and AI research. He should be able to discover ways to advance AI technology.
Research Scientist	The person should be expert in Applied Mathematics, Machine Learning, Deep Learning and Computational Statistics. He/she is expected to have an advanced degree in Computer Science or an advanced degree in a related field supported by experience.
Software Engineer	The person should be able to develop programs on which AI tools function.
Data Mining and Analysis	The person should be capable of finding anomalies, patterns, etc. within large data sets to predict outcomes.
Machine Learning Engineer	The person should be capable of using data to design, build and manage ML software applications.
Data Scientist	The person should be able to collect, analyse and interpret datasets.
Business Intelligence (BI) Developer	The person should be able to analyse complex data sets to identify business and market trends.
Big Data Engineer/Architect	Develop systems that allow businesses to communicate and collate data.

Let us have a look on some AI using companies in India that are much popular in the AI job market.

- Amazon
- Facebook
- Apple
- Google
- Accenture
- IBM
- Microsoft
- Baker Hughes
- PepsiCo
- Casetext

Practical Skills Required

For All Jobs

- Programming languages (Python, R, Java are the most necessary)
- Software development skills like Eclipse and IntelliJ
- Linear algebra and statistics

- Signal processing techniques
- Neural network architectures
- Query Languages like SQL, MySQL

Job Type	Qualifications/Skills Required
Data Mining and Analysis	• B. Tech (I.T.) or M. Tech or Doctoral Degree in Computer Science or MCA or Master Degree in Computer Science or Mathematics
Machine Learning Engineer	• B. Tech (I.T.) or M. Tech or Doctoral Degree in Computer Science or MCA or Master Degree in Computer Science or Mathematics • Python or Java Expertise
Data Scientist	• M. Tech or Doctoral Degree in Computer Science • Expertise in SAS and R, Python, Hadoop, Cloud tools
Business Intelligence Developer	• BCA/B. Tech/MCA • Experience in data warehouse design, data mining, SQL queries, SQL Server Reporting Services (SSRS) and SQL Server Integration Services (SSIS) are preferred.
Research Scientist	• M. Sc/M. Tech or doctoral degree in Computer Science • Experience in, artificial intelligence, machine learning, knowledge of algorithms, and distributed computing.
Software Engineer	• B.Tech (IT)/MCA • Experience in Software Development Tools
Big Data Engineer/Architect	• B. Tech (IT)/MCA • Experience in databases, query languages

TO DEVELOP EFFECTIVE COMMUNICATION AND COLLABORATIVE WORK SKILLS

Collaboration means working together with one or more people to complete a project or task or develop ideas or processes.

In the workplace, collaboration occurs when two or more people work together towards a common goal of the company. Workplace collaboration requires:

- interpersonal skills
- communication skills
- knowledge sharing
- strategy

Working as a team brings greater productivity. It also creates healthy relationships between employees.

Employees working together are more effective and efficient than those work on the same project alone. Collaborating also increases motivation and level of engagement at work.

Sharing ideas and brainstorming is helpful for developing better solutions to complex challenges. There are many ways to collaborate effectively at work and the skills and techniques you rely on when you collaborate can lead to greater efficiency and success.

AI Changes the Way We Work and Collaborate

Digital tools have changed the way we work, meet, collaborate and innovate. Smart machines are bringing new intelligent automation to the workplace as well as our personal devices.

Let us focus on recent advances in natural language processing (NLP) and machine learning. These AI applications have entered the modern workplace to improve efficiency at the workplace and meetings.

AI works best when used with human intelligence. A new collective intelligence will make us collaboration experts.

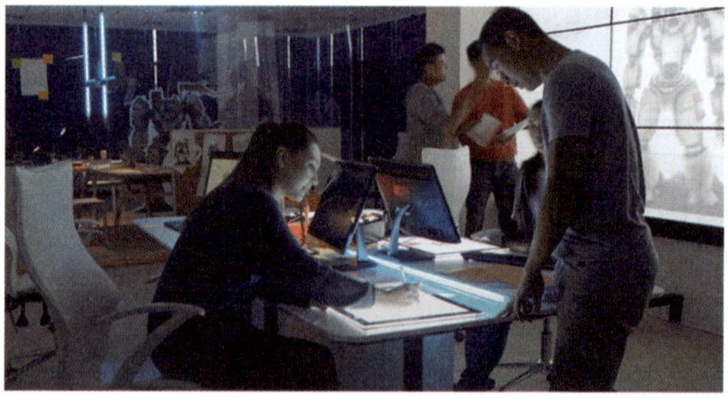

AI for Pre-Meeting Efficiency

AI has the power to improve meetings with smart scheduling, auto-composition of messages, intelligent risk management and self-healing. This starts teamwork and focuses efforts on collaboration.

- **Smart Scheduling :** Sometimes coordinating the meeting time, attendees and agenda can take a long time. AI can optimize this process.

  By applying Natural Language Processing, NLP, AI responds to commands by voice or text and connects to calendar applications:

  - to set appointments
  - to invite participants
  - to locate the best meeting room location
  - to track responses.

  By applying Machine Learning Algorithms with NLP, AI will learn:

» who should be part of the meeting
» the best time and locations for the meeting
» predict preferences of attendees.

For Example:

AI will know the meeting organizer prefers afternoon working sessions, but not immediately following budget meetings.

- **Auto-Compose Messaging:** Auto-composition is an essential addition to smart scheduling.

  AI bots are helpful in:

  » composing calendar invitations
  » writing email messages to attendees with the meeting agenda
  » attaching notes from the last session if available.

  Today, auto-composition completes sentences and recommends appropriate replies for email messages.

- **Identifying and Managing Quality and Security Risks:** System and network variability can affect meeting quality by dropping packets in a video call, hindering content sharing or delaying audio streams.

  AI can identify and resolve these common faults. Machine learning responds to:

  » network and system anomalies
  » throttling bandwidth
  » changes in configurations

  AI helps in removing faults at its own without disrupting the meeting or by alerting the help desk.

  AI-powered automation saves IT and facilities teams hours of time otherwise spent tracking and resolving routine service tickets. It frees up time for more strategic support tasks.

- **AI for In-Meeting Productivity:** Once AI takes care of meeting preparation—coordinating people and technology for collaboration—it will join the meeting.

  AI will take on several collaboration roles, from virtual digital assistant, to self-service help desk, to real-time, self-healing, system agent. It will help in collaborating more effortlessly and meaningfully.

Voice-Activated Control

Some of the most enticing AI skills for meetings are by voice-activated controls. These include conversational AI or NLP to accept the requests, identify the speaker and transcribe commands from speech to text.

The human voice replaces other user interfaces, like touchscreen panels, occupancy sensors, keyboard strokes and mouse clicks.

Use of voice enabled search queries during meetings is very helpful.

For Example:

We may ask our AI-enabled, voice-activated assistant, "Which services the X company is providing?"

AI will translate the query, know its context, conduct the search and return results by displaying possible answers on the meeting screen.

AI eliminates connectivity challenges that delay meeting starts and increases teamwork with simple, voice-activated search queries. It will save hours of collaboration and improve project results.

- **Virtual Digital Assistant:** Having a virtual digital assistant as a project team member allows the participants to focus on creative problem solving.

  AI itself manages meeting workflows.

  AI-powered discovery will reduce research time and also gives new ideas. The virtual digital assistant will assign tasks with deadlines, track task completion and report project progress.

  Working with virtual digital assistants Google Assistant and IBM Watson in meetings saves project and creates a collective intelligence. The collective intelligence will accelerate team output.

VIRTUAL DIGITAL ASSISTANTS

Google Assistant	by Google
Corotona	by Microsoft
Mycroft	by Mycroft AI team
Siri	by Apple
Amazon Echo	by Amazon
Bixby	by Samsung
Lucida	by Clarity Lab
Cubic	by Cubic Robotics
BlackBerry Assistant	by BlackBerry
Maluuba	by Maluuba

Self-Service Help Desk

AI chatbots are already at the front lines of customer service. Zendesk is a leader in AI-enabled customer experience, using natural language processing and deep learning to continually improve service levels.

With conversational AI, users will ask for help during a meeting, through voice or text. AI will transcribe the request. Queries will be quickly solved by the chatbot which responds from the knowledge base. If the solution is not available, it routes the request to the most qualified help desk technician.

Accessibility

AI tools provide access to collaboration for those participants who left or could not attend the meeting for a disability, such as hearing or vision impairment.

With NLP and machine learning, meetings will be automatically transcribed and translated to any language in real time to allow all team members to fully participate in meetings with ease.

Sentiment Analysis

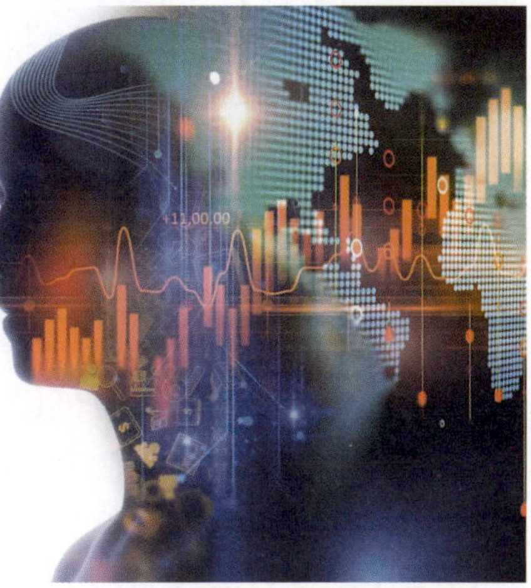

The task of sentiment analysis involves taking a piece of text, whether it is a sentence, a comment or an entire document and returning a "score" that measures how positive or negative the text is.

AI is making progress in estimating human sentiment. It is coaching call-centre agents while handling customer inquiries.

AI reads voice modulations to detect the expression. With these tools, AI may perceive the sentiment of meeting participants, their level of engagement in the meeting and their satisfaction with the technology.

We can see applications of AI-powered sentiment analysis to broadly advise IT, HR and facilities managers about which meeting rooms are preferred and which technology causes excessive frustration or benefit, for users.

There are two basic techniques for sentiment analysis:

- **Rule-Based Sentiment Analysis:** This technique uses a dictionary of words labelled by sentiment to determine the sentiment of a sentence.
- **Machine Learning (ML) Based Sentiment Analysis:** This technique is Machine Learning (ML) based. Here, we train an ML model to recognize the sentiment based on the words and their order using a sentiment-labelled training set.

AI Improves Collaboration and Workplace Experience

When AI eliminates the most common operational difficulties like;

- meeting scheduling
- technology availability
- knowledge access
- project management

People can Truly Collaborate.

Teamwork will happen when people focus on creative problem solving.

Projects have stronger business outcomes when AI is working in the background. It is helpful for productive meetings and provides relevant information that speeds decision making and improves results.

AI creates team collaboration. It also frees departments from:

- continuous monitoring
- maintenance
- management of meeting spaces and technology.

This enables employees to focus on more complex issues, like security. With enhanced teamwork, efficiency and creativity, the overall workplace experience becomes great.

AI benefits extend beyond real and virtual meetings to other workplace environments like smart buildings, IoT, research laboratories and training rooms.

COLLABORATIVE LEARNING WITH AI

Collaborative learning (CL) is an educational approach of teaching and learning that involves groups of learners working together to solve a problem, complete a task or create a product.

Educators can use AI for collaborative learning in the following manner:

Group Formation

AI can study large volumes of data about every student. This data can include their:

- academic performance
- attendance
- style of working.

Using such data, AI can divide students into well-balanced groups to complete different projects. Such groups may include students who have an equal level of understanding about a subject.

Even educators can customize AI systems to form groups that consist of students with different levels of academic performance. This can help students in using their own unique talents in a group.

Therefore, AI can allow educators to create optimal groups of students for every project. Similar tools can be used in companies to form groups for different projects.

Evaluation of Collaborative Abilities

AI systems can evaluate each student's level of collaboration by studying large volumes of data about them.

Based on the evaluation of AI systems, educators can suggest ways to increase collaboration or correct undesirable things in the learning process.

Therefore, educators can help students in improving their collaborative abilities.

Virtual Agents

AI can be used to create virtual agents that can help students in group projects.

These virtual agents can answer their queries and behave like a teacher who can teach them.

With these applications, virtual agents can help in group projects. Such virtual agents can be quite useful in educational games and online courses. Virtual agents can test every student's understanding of the subject matter by asking questions. Virtual agents can make the learning experience more informative and interactive.

Monitoring Conversation

During group discussions and debates, monitoring the conversations of different groups is difficult. AI systems can monitor conversations of many groups using recording devices.

These AI programs can alert educators in case a group's conversation diverts from the topic.

Learning Gaps

Students lagging behind in a lesson or a subject is a common thing in schools. The reasons for such learning gaps can be:

- an inability to grasp new concepts
- difficulty to study material
- ineffective teaching methods.

Understanding the exact reason behind lagging of a student, can be quite difficult. AI systems can study large datasets to identify such students and complexities in the curriculum.

For this, AI systems can use Natural Language Processing to analyse the content and context of study materials. Based on this analysis, educators can create personalized learning plans or assignments to bridge learning gaps.

AI-based collaborative learning will improve each student's communication and collaboration skills.

Such technologies can help educational institutions in improving the quality of education significantly.

AI FOR ADVERTISING

AI technologies are very deep to understand, but you do not need a full technical understanding of AI to take advantage of it as a marketer and advertiser.

- The most advanced AI learns from huge amount of data sets and improves its analysis, predictions and recommendations over a time. From this, many outcomes are possible, especially in the world of advertising.
- AI is able to analyse huge sets of data about online advertising and can create an excellent copy of the ad based on its best prediction. It is able to interpret data about how consumers interact with advertising, then use those insights to optimize campaigns to perform better.
- AI is already being used to regulate the ads which are bought by a company or it can create or optimize the ad you click on.
- Performance optimization is one of the keys for AI in advertising. Machine learning algorithms are used to analyse how your ad performs on a specific platform. It offers recommendations on how to improve performance.
- AI-powered systems can create ads on the basis of goals set by a company.
- Ad targeting is also an important thing. It also includes use of platforms like Facebook, LinkedIn, Amazon and Google.

Overview of the Artificial Intelligence Market in India

The AI market in India till now (the following is an approximate data upto 2021), has been dominated by the MNC Technology firms. Only Domestic IT firms have shown some significant progress in investment.

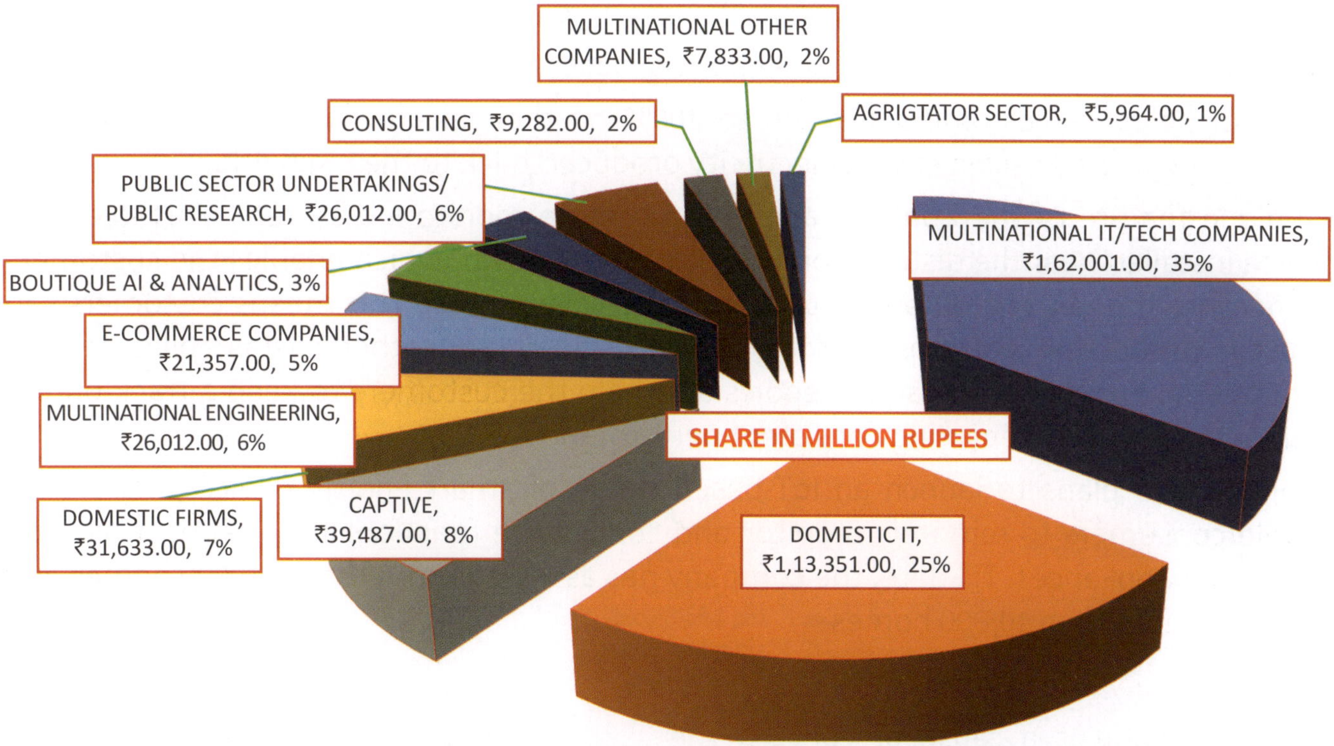

India has a big stake in the AI revolution. The leading technology institutions in the country, such as IITs, NITs and IIITs, have the ability to be the cradle of AI researchers and start-ups. In order to solve social problems, Indian start-ups are growing and developing AI solutions in education, health, financial services and other fields.

INSPIRING START-UPS, COMPANIES OR COMMUNITIES WHERE AI HAS BEEN INVOLVED IN REAL-LIFE

ZunRoof: Solar Rooftops using Image processing and Virtual Reality

Rooftop solar start-up ZunRoof calls itself a home-tech firm that uses image processing, virtual reality (VR), Internet of Things (IoT) and data analytics to generate solar power from rooftops and provide control of every appliance in the house.

How They are Using Technology to Solve Problems?

The firm was founded in June 2016 (Bengaluru).

Driven by image processing, virtual reality, AI, 3D layouts and data analytics, the ZunRoof app offers homeowners a free platform to upload images of their rooftop, to design an optimal solar rooftop system.

Once the images have been uploaded, the app helps in recommending optimal system size, positioning and inclination of solar panels, based on your electricity requirements.

ZunRoof helps its customers save up to 100% on their electricity bills and also make monthly income by selling excess electricity produced back to the main grid.

A unique feature of the ZunRoof app is the remote monitoring system. This is an IoT device installed near the distribution box of the household, which enables the customers to measure the net energy production from the solar panels. This means customers can monitor production patterns of their rooftop panels and other sustainability-related parameters. Further, the analysis reports also help the customers to keep a track on the maintenance visit for ensuring consistent performance.

ZunRoof also plans to launch an IoT-based range of smart energy devices, which will enable consumers to remotely monitor and control the functionality of almost all their household appliances. Till date, the company has assessed more than 150,000 homes and designed more than 10,000 homes.

Blue Sky Analytics

Climate change is a cause of concern the world over. Over the years, with the growth in industries and extreme pollution across cities, global warming has led to a huge meltdown in polar caps. However, Blue Sky Analytics, a Gurugram-based space-tech start-up is providing high-resolution and high-frequency environmental data to global stakeholders using its in-house proprietary AI-enabled solutions.

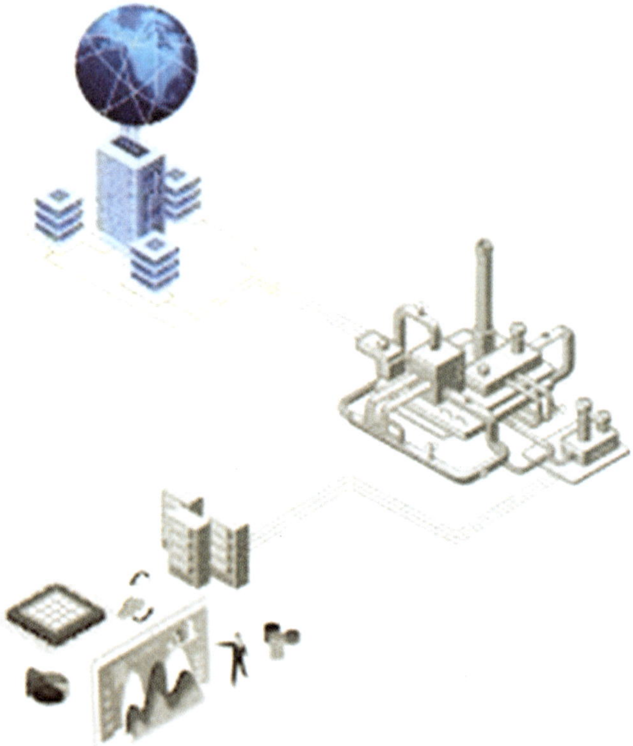

Blue Sky Analytics is a geospatial data intelligence start-up, leveraging satellite data with IoT to provide accessible, high resolution, high frequency and near real-time data. The start-up is on a mission to combat the menace of air pollution and enable informed decision making.

Can you believe satellites orbiting 400 miles above the Earth's surface send data that can be used to monitor particles that are less than 1/10th the width of human hair. Blue Sky Analytics provides its users contextualised air quality information, real-time air quality data with next three-day predictions, long time series historical data (five years), comparing air quality of multiple stations, user engagement *via* gamification, news aggregator, etc.

ACTIVITY

NEURAL STYLE TRANSFER IN TENSORFLOW

One of the most exciting developments in deep learning is to come out recently with artistic style transfer or the ability to create a new image, known as a pastiche, based on two input images: one representing the artistic style and one representing the content.

Neural style transfer is an optimization technique used to take two images—a content image and a style reference image (such as an artwork by a famous painter)—and blend them together so the output image looks like the content image, but "painted" in the style of the style reference image.

In general, when the input image is passed neural network, hidden layers act as a collection of filters, which extract certain features from the image. It is possible to manipulate content and style of that image and therefore, style can be transferred to other images

It can be understood easily through the examples below:

Original Content Image

Style Photo

Stylized Photo

Original Content Image

Style Photo

Stylized Photo

https://www.tensorflow.org/lite/examples/style_transfer/overview

There are similar other applications for transferring the styles of images into new one.

For Example:

Explore the site https://github.com/NVIDIA/FastPhotoStyle

Content Photo

Style Photo

Stylized Content

ACTIVITY

BALLOON DEBATE

TOPIC: FUTURISTIC JOB OPPORTUNITIES

You have already learnt that a balloon debate is a debate in which a number of speakers take part and everyone tries to win the vote of an audience. The audience is asked to imagine that the participants in the debate are flying in a hot-air balloon and suddenly the hot balloon which has started leaking. This balloon will sink down if all the speakers (except one speaker) are not thrown outside.

Each speaker tries to make a case why he should not be thrown out of the balloon. Each participant speaks on a topic. Here, suppose our topic is Artificial Intelligence. The speakers will have to speak on the benefits and limitations of AI.

Class Situation: The class is all together up in a hot-air balloon, which has sudden leak. It is losing air and threatening to crash. All but one must jump out to lighten the burden. Only one student can survive (or one group of students will survive, if groups have been formed).

Each has to justify why he should stay in the balloon and others not.

Topic : Impact of AI in Futuristic Job Opportunities

Purpose: To be familiar with the impact of AI on Futuristic Job Opportunities.

We are going to debate about the boon and bane of various AI applications in the different areas. This will be a group debate (Four *versus* Four). The same theme will be given to two different teams.

Teams will be named as:

- Team speaking in favour of Artificial Intelligence: Affirmative Team (Team A)
- Team speaking against Artificial Intelligence: Rebuttal Team (Team B)

One team of four speakers will be asked to speak in favour of the theme "Impact of AI in Futuristic Job Opportunities" and the other team will be asked to speak against the theme.

The debate will go theme by theme wherein each member of the team will get a minute to speak.

The first speaker of the Affirmative Team will start the debate after which the first speaker of the rebuttal team will put his points.

In this manner, each speaker will get a minute to speak and finally one team will be chosen to be thrown out of the balloon debate depending upon how convincing their points were. The speaker who speaks more than a minute will get his team disqualified. You will get 10 minutes to prepare your points. And your time starts now!"

This is hot-balloon like situation.

Reflect and Discuss:

- How do you think that AI will affect futuristic job opportunities?
- AI will create more job gaps and create wealth inqualities.

Discuss this with your peers and write your views:

____

____

____

____

____

EXERCISE

Performance Assessment, Review and Analysis

Fill in the Blanks with Given Hints

1. Chatbots are ________________.
2. The branch of AI related with speech is ________________.
3. Chatbots are being used in ________________ and other ________________.

HINTS

NLP, Banks, Offices, Robots

Write T for True and F for False

1. Sentimental analysis can work without datasets. [ ]
2. Machine learning is used in Sentimental Analysis. [ ]
3. Artificial intelligence is not supportive for workplace collaboration. [ ]
4. AI is helpful in collaborative learning. [ ]
5. All robots are self-ruling. [ ]
6. A robot can do only that work for which it is programmed. [ ]
7. Robotics and AI are not the same things. [ ]

Multiple Choice Questions

Tick [✓] the best alternatives.

1. In which area, the AI is superior than Human ______________.
   (a) Planning [ ] (b) Thinking [ ]
   (c) Judgement [ ] (d) Speed [ ]
2. AI is ______________ in collaborate learning.
   (a) Not helpful [ ] (b) Partially helpful [ ]
   (c) Helpful [ ] (d) None of these [ ]
3. Sentimental analysis analyses ______________.
   (a) Words [ ] (b) Images [ ]
   (c) Graphs [ ] (d) None of these [ ]
4. Converting a content photo and style photo into stylized photo is the process of ______________.
   (a) Image editing [ ] (b) Natural Language Processing [ ]
   (c) Neural Network [ ] (d) Artistic Network [ ]

5. Bixby virtual assistant is a product of ______________ .

(a) Microsoft [ ] (b) Samsung [ ]

(c) Apple [ ] (d) Google [ ]

Competency Based Questions

1. Job Ad Creating activity: Learners to create a job advertisement for a firm describing the nature of job available and the skill-set required for it 10 years down the line. They need to figure out how AI is going to transform the nature of jobs and create the Ad accordingly.
2. After studying the chapter, you now know the academic qualifications and other skills required for the AI related jobs. Your brother who is studying in 12th class now wants to become a Research Scientist in the field of Artificial Intelligence. Help him to choose for the higher course after 12th class.

Answer the Following Questions

1. Write any two skills required for jobs in future.

____

____

2. Write two areas where Artificial Intelligence is not superior to human.

____

____

3. Write any two benefits of AI in collaborative working at workplace.

____

____

4. Write any two benefits of AI in collaborative learning.

____

____

5. What are the benefits of AI in the field of advertising?

____

____

LAB ACTIVITY

For Students

- Make a presentation on the uses of AI in collaborative skills.

Group Discussion:

- Collaborative Learning
- Sentiment Analysis

For Teachers

- As we dig more and more, the benefits of AI surface up. You may discuss other fields where AI can be helpful without posing any threat to human employment.

5

AI ETHICS

Introduction

With the use of every technology, ethical issues are involved.

However, AI is a powerful tool but it too has problems related to ethics. In order to ensure it can do good, we first have to understand the risks and try to improve the things related to ethics so that the technology should prove beneficial for the users and humanity at large. Let us study the AI ethics issues.

Learning Outcomes

- To understand and reflect on the ethical issues around AI.
- To gain awareness around AI bias and AI access.
- To let the students, analyse the advantages and disadvantages of Artificial Intelligence.

Coverage:

Ethical issues around AI, AI bias and AI access. Advantages and disadvantages of Artificial Intelligence.

IMPLICATIONS OF AI TECHNOLOGY

AI or artificial intelligence is a very broad term that includes simple exciting things from Apple's Siri and Amazon's Alexa, to more complex things like autonomous vehicles and robotics.

AI is growing in importance every year, with new forms and uses.

AI could be an incredible tool if we fully explore it. Artificial intelligence is very important because it may one day completely change the face of society with an impact on the job scene (old jobs vanishing and new job opportunities evolving).

Some people find AI as unsettling thing. The idea that something can get so close to being a human, but only consists of codes and hardware, is a disturbing thought for them.

- Super computers have the ability to recall and analyse more data and gather information faster than any one human could.
- Robots, depending on the purpose they serve, can be hundreds of times physically stronger than a human.

If the above two are combined into one creation think what can happen in the field of computer technology. AI fields are continuing to grow, with new advances being made all the time.

Strong artificial intelligence is achieved when a system can take information from the outside world and learn by itself and build an awareness similar or superior to that of a human.

AI can change our society and it can affect the job scene both in positive and negative manner. In general, AI or robots can replace almost any job a human can do.

An increasing number of people feel that their ability to make a living will be affected by artificial workers (AI systems) in the near future.

Younger people who have good analytical, problem-solving and decision-making skills are away from any threat of the AI.

Artificial Intelligence is still in its starting form and is yet to reach the point of mass adoption. As such it is difficult to predict the extent to which it will redefine the workplace or the jobs of the young professionals within it.

ETHICAL ISSUES AROUND AI

Ethics is also defined as the discipline dealing with right *versus* wrong and the moral obligations and duties of humans.

What are the moral obligations and duties of creators of AI?

These two include:

- How right the AI system is?
- How fair and how just is an algorithm?

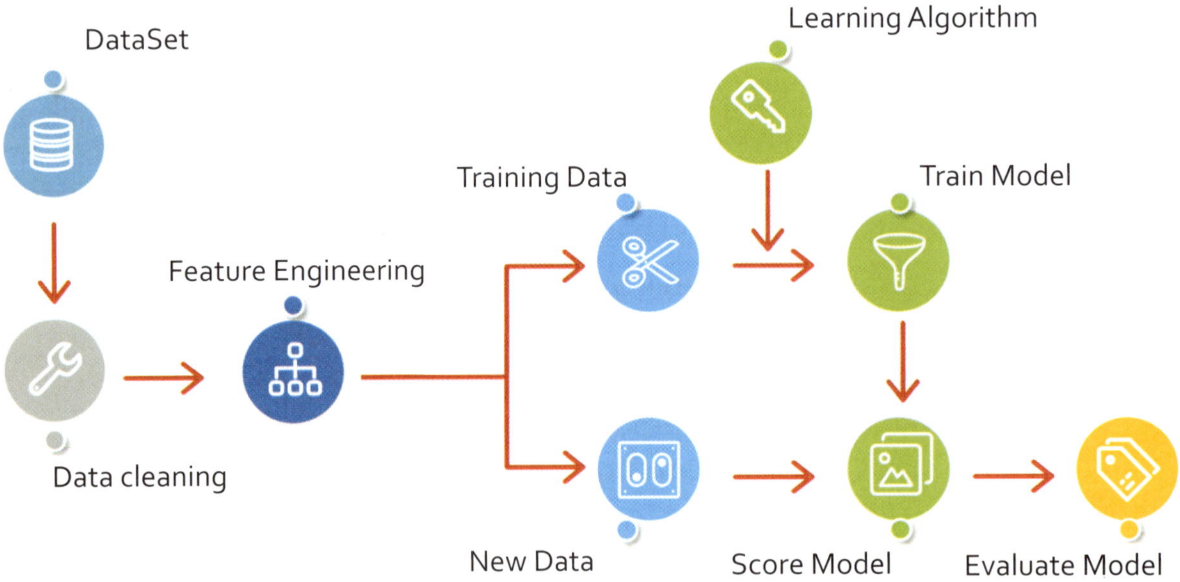

- How fair and how just is the output of the algorithm?
- What is the outcome of the algorithm?
- What is the impact of the outcome on the society?

All the above things are related with AI ethics.

We can simply say that AI is based on datasets, models and predictions.

Based on these points, we have to judge the following things:

Note the fact

- Feature Engineering is the process of selecting, manipulating and transforming raw data into features that can be used in supervised learning.
- Score Model is an algorithm which outputs a predicted value for a class and probability of the predicted value.
- Train Model is a model that simply learns good values for all the weights and the biases from labelled examples.
- Evaluate Model is a model to understand a machine learning model's performance, as well as its strengths and weaknesses.

- Bias (whether it is unbiased)
- Fairness (whether it is fair)
- Transparency (whether is it transparent)
- Interpreting – ability (whether it is understanding correctly)
- Explaining – ability (whether it is explaining the query correctly)
- Accountability (who is accountable if the system is biased?)

Various issues are linked with the AI ethics.

In Using Machines

• Safety	(Whether it is safe to use the machine in all conditions. For example; using a robot should always be safe and it should not harm human).
• Human-AI interaction	(Whether human-machine interaction is user-friendly and easy. Does a machine responds to the human queries in a friendly manner?).  

• Cyber Security and Malicious Use	(As more reliance is placed on AI, the importance of cyber security will increase. Security must be a top priority for all. Whether cyber laws are powerful.) 
• Privacy, Control and Surveillance	(Whether the AI system are secure in terms of privacy. Is there proper controlling element for the AI systems? Are AI systems under proper surveillance?) 

Impacts of AI

- Automation (Whether AI system is able to do complete automation)
- Job loss (What is the impact of jobs?)
- Impact to Democracy and Civil Rights (Whether using the AI system will affect the democracy and civil rights of the user).

AI IN SCHOOLS

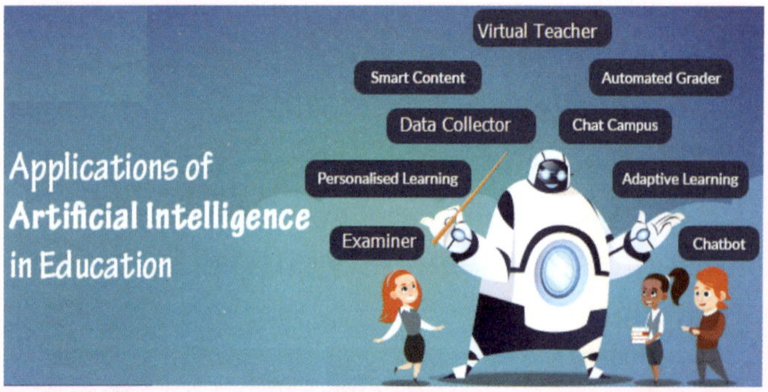

Artificial intelligence is gaining attraction in schools. A school environment supported by Artificial Intelligence (AI) systems is most probably the near future. However, its implementation is not easier and calls for addressing several related issues.

Let us understand the risks of using artificial intelligence in schools and study the necessary safety measures to mitigate these risks.

Risks of Using Artificial Intelligence in Schools

- The solutions delivered through AI may be biased as it is dependent on the developers' educational ideas.
- The Artificial Intelligence may only recommend the content that are based on hits and likes and not based on quality content.
- There is a lack of meaningful teacher-interaction and therefore, the nurturing of students may not be dependent on students' emotion.
- It is thought that AI in schools will reduce costs of teaching, but it may prove costly as teachers will become more costly considering the emotional aspects.

Safety Measures to be Adopted while Using Artificial Intelligence in Schools

- There is a need for teacher's intervention in all aspects of data collection, its analysis and remedial measures before the student is targeted.
- AI systems should be easy and safe to use.
- It should not be hurting the emotions of students.
- It should not be hurting the students physically.
- It should not share the data of the children to any outside agency.

Let us discuss on some of the points related to the AI ethics in details.

1. Job Loss and Wealth Inequality

People fear that AI is playing a negative role on their jobs. They blame AI for future job loss. They think if there are fully developed AI systems in the society, many people will lose their jobs and quite possibly their livelihood.

It is a rough estimate that by the year 2030, about 800 million people will lose their jobs to AI-driven robots.

Not as such that AI will create job loss, AI may create more jobs. After all, people will be tasked with creating these robots and then manage them in the future. It would not be difficult to find a job for the qualified person in the field of AI.

The Issue Related to Job Loss is Wealth Inequality.

Consider that an economic system requires workers to produce a product or service with their payment based on hourly-wage system. The company pays wages, taxes and other expenses. With the left-over profits, the company puts these profits back into production, training and creating more business to further increase profits. In this way, the company generates more jobs and the economy continues to grow.

But what Happens If We Introduce AI into the Economy?

Robots do not get paid on hourly basis and they do not have to pay taxes. They can contribute at a level of 100% with low cost of working. This opens the door for owners to keep more company profits generated by their AI workforce. It leads to greater wealth inequality.

Those individuals and companies who have the means to pay for AIs will be getting richer.

2. AI is not Perfect—It can Make Mistakes

AI systems can make mistakes and machine learning takes time to become useful. If trained well using good data, AI systems can perform well.

If we feed bad data to AI systems or make errors with internal programming, the AI systems can be harmful.

Microsoft's AI chatbot, Tay, was released on Twitter in 2016. In less than one day, due to the information it was receiving and learning from other Twitter users, the robot learned to emit racist words and propaganda. Microsoft shut down the chatbot immediately.

AIs make mistakes:

- But do they make more or less mistakes than humans?
- How many lives have humans taken with mistaken decisions?
- Is it better or worse when an AI makes the same mistake?

Let us understand and reflect on the ethical issues around AI.

Let us discuss about robot morality:

- A robot must not harm a human being.
- A robot must follow orders given by human beings.
- A robot must protect its own existence.

What is Required in Commercial Robots?

- **Safety:** There must be mechanisms for an operator to handle, control and limit a robot's autonomy.
- **Security:** There must be a password or other keys to avoid wrong and illegal use of a robot.
- **Traceability:** Like aircraft, robots should have a "black box" to record and document their own behaviour.
- **Identifiability:** Robots should have registration number similar to cars.
- **Privacy policy:** Software and hardware should be used to encrypt and protect the sensitive data with the password that the robot needs to save.

3. AI and Gender Equality

AI systems may have implications for gender equality. They may reflect existing societal biases and even show the large effect. Most AI systems are built using datasets. These datasets reflect the real world; which can be unfair and discriminatory also.

Such systems can be dangerous because they perpetuate gender inequalities in society.

These inequalities are the result of how machines learn. Machine learning relies on the data with which it is fed. Particular attention is needed to promote gender-sensitive data collection.

In Amazon's hiring tool, the bias emerged because the tool was learning from previous Amazon candidates. Those candidates were mostly male. The system had learnt that male applicants should be preferred over female applicants.

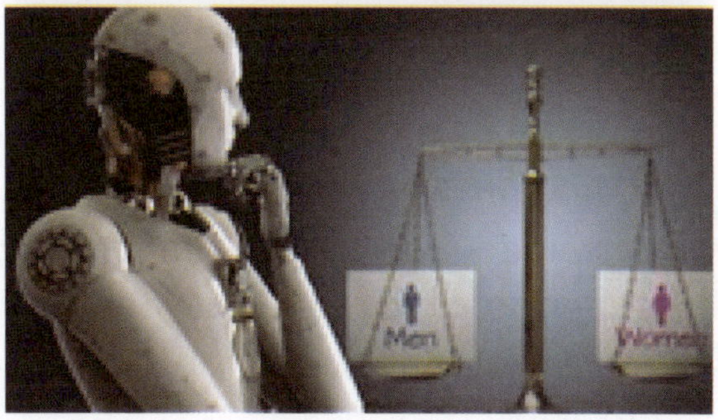

Paying attention to biased data would therefore limit the blind spot and will create AI systems best suited and designed for both men and women.

Points to Note in Gender Inequalities

- It is important to note that gender inequalities begin at the early stages of designing AI systems. The gender inequality is well known from wage gaps to promotions.
- There is low share of women in the AI workforce.
- The share of women is also low in digital skills development in general. It means that women's voices fade away in the decision-making processes for design and development of AI systems.

AI BIAS

A bias means remarkably different things in different *contexts. AI bias is an anomaly in the output of machine learning algorithms, due to lack of data or poor quality of data and the assumptions made during the algorithm development process.*

Machine Learning and Artificial Intelligence (ML/AI) algorithms are simply tools for continuing the patterns you show them. If you show them bad patterns, they will reflect the bad behaviour.

Bias does not come from ML/AI algorithms, it comes from people. Machine does not think itself. It is up to us humans to do the thinking for them.

Bias can creep in at various stages of the deep-learning process. The standard practices in Computer Science are not designed to detect it.

AI has become increasingly important in facial and voice recognition systems. These recognition systems are business implications that directly impact people. These systems are vulnerable to biases and errors introduced by their human makers.

Moreover, the data used to train these AI systems itself can have biases.

For instance, facial recognition algorithms developed by Microsoft, IBM and Megvii; all had biases in detecting people's gender. These AI systems were able to detect the gender of white people more accurately than gender of darker-skin people.

Similarly, Amazon.com's termination of AI hiring and recruitment is another example which shows that AI cannot be fair. The algorithm preferred male candidates over female. This was because Amazon's system was trained with data collected over a 10-year period which was provided by majority of male candidates.

Can AI Become Biased?

Intelligent machines do not have a moral values or principles like human has. Even moral values and principles of humans sometimes do not benefit humanity as a whole. How can we ensure that AI agents do not have the same flaws as their creators?

The biases people carry in their everyday lives can be reflected. Such biases can even be amplified through the development and use of AI systems.

For Example:

'*Gendering*' of digital assistants may reflect understandings of women as obeying and compliant servant. Female voices are routinely chosen as personal assistance bots mainly fulfilling customer service jobs. The majority of bots in professional services coded as male voices.

The notion of 'gender' in AI systems is often a simple choice either male or female.

If AI develops a certain bias towards race, gender, religion or society, then the fault will lie mostly on how it was taught and trained.

Therefore, people who work in AI research, need to keep bias in mind when determining what data to use.

How AI Bias Happens?

People often tell their views about AI bias by blaming on biased training data. The reality is something different; bias can creep in long before the data is collected. A bias can also happen at many other stages of the deep-learning process.

From research, it has been found that more than 180 human biases are there and any one of which can affect our decisions.

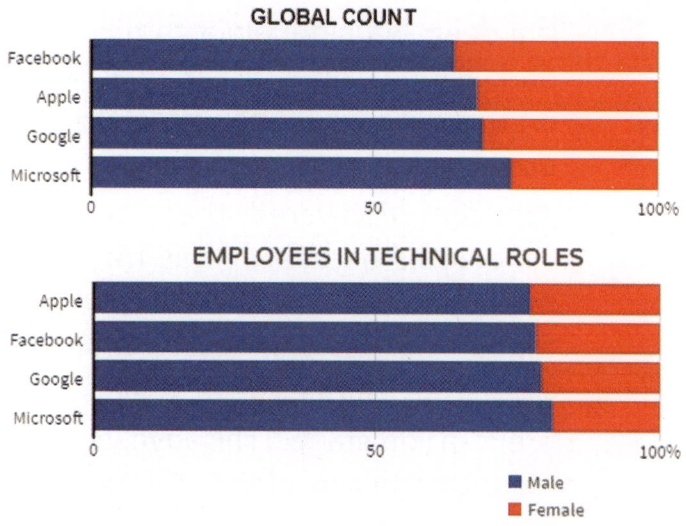

As human and AI work together to make decisions, researchers are looking at ways to ensure human bias does not affect the data or algorithms used to arrive at those decisions.

Identifying and removing bias in AI systems is essential to building trust between humans and machines that learn.

Let us focus on the following points:

- **Framing the Problem :** The first thing computer scientists do when they create a deep-learning model is to decide what they actually want it to do.

  For Example:

  A credit card company might want to predict creditworthiness of a customer.

  To know the credit-worthiness, the company must decide:

  ›› whether it wants to maximize its profit margins or

  ›› maximize the number of those loans that are repaid.

  It could then define credit-worthiness within the context of that goal.

  The problem is that such decisions are made for various business reasons and not on fairness or discrimination.

  If the algorithm discovers that giving out unimportant loans has increased the profits of the company, then it will say that the category of giving this type of loan is better. It will end up with inappropriate behaviour even if that was not the company's intention to give such types of unimportant loans.

- **Collecting the Data :** There are *two* main ways of bias being crept in training data:

  The data you collect is away from reality,

  or

  It reflects existing opinions that are not based on reason or actual experience.

  For Example:

  If a deep-learning, algorithm is fed with more photos of light-skinned faces than dark-skinned faces, then what will happen? The face recognition system based on this data would be worse at recognizing darker-skinned faces. *This means, the data you have collected is away from reality*.

  Amazon discovered that its internal recruiting tool was dismissing female candidates because it was trained on historical hiring decisions, which favoured men over women. *Therefore, such results show that the data reflects the opinions that are not based on reason or actual experience*.

- **Preparing the Data :** It is possible that a bias could introduce during the data preparation stage. This involves selection of attributes (properties) you want the algorithm to consider.

  For Example:

  In modelling credit-worthiness, an *attribute* could be:

  - age of the applicant
  - income
  - number of paid-off loans
  - CIBIL report (a report which a branch of bank generates online whether the applicant is good enough in credit-worthiness)
  - security available with the applicant.

  Choosing which attributes to consider or ignore can significantly influence prediction accuracy of your model. It is called the art of deep learning.

  An important principle, for both humans and machines, is to avoid bias and therefore prevent discrimination. Bias in AI system mainly occurs due to weak data or the insufficient algorithmic model.

  Therefore, when we work to develop AI systems:

  - It is important to train these systems with unbiased data.
  - The data should be collected with a mixed group of people and not from a particular gender/group.
  - The data to be fed in the AI systems must be tested again and again for accuracy.
  - It is equally important to develop algorithms that can be easily explained.

AI is a tool for recognizing things in large amounts of data.

Therefore, AI is the thing, we are trying to remove bias from. It is also the tool we can use to recognize bias in the systems we build. It also helps in recognizing our own biases.

What is Being Done to Remove Biases?

- **Getting Broader Data:** Researchers are creating different methods to reduce bias in AI without reducing the accuracy of results.

  The simplest approach for solving bias issues is to begin by gathering diverse datasets that inform our machine learning models. Diverse data is the absolute starting point for creating AI.

- **Datasheets :** This is a method for tracking about. The datasheets focus what did this data measure and how was it measured?

  Therefore, if you have to purchase a dataset, the author of that dataset would include a standardized datasheet. This document captures aspects of the research that play into:

  → its contextual nature

  → ethical nature

  → biased nature

  Anyone purchasing that data can be aware of the above qualities before using it.

  Microsoft has been doing a significant amount of work in this area. It is developing a tool that can detect bias in artificial intelligence algorithms. The goal of this tool is to help the businesses using AI without the risk of discriminating against certain people.

- **Bias Auditing :** These are the tools that review machine learning algorithms. They present reports that consider various aspects of the data being given to the systems and how the data and tools are affecting the results.

  Users can then test solutions to see how they could improve the success ratios and decide which solution to apply.

  One of the most well-known examples of a tool is by Pymetrics (Pymetrics bias solution for employers) called Audit AI, which can examine the output of any machine learning technique. Audit AI is designed to detect bias, primarily in Human Resource (HR) tools. But if there is any imbalance in algorithm, then it is the role of creator.

- **Digital Decisioning Platforms for Bias and Ethics :** Decisioning platforms help users in quickly making the decisions to improve their models for bias.

  This can be done by them by applying machine learning models combined with natural language to provide automated insights and recommendations from the AI to the user.

They are different from bias auditing tools. They go beyond reporting results. Their outputs are designed as recommendations. They will automate the application of any approved suggestions at their own.

- **Conversational Discovery Assistants :** IBM's Project Debater is the first AI system that can debate humans on complex topics.

  It takes massive texts, constructs a well-structured speech on a given topic, delivers it with clarity and purpose and rebuts its opponent.

  Project Debater will help people to reason by providing solid evidence-based arguments and limiting the influence of emotion, bias or ambiguity.

  IBM's Project Debater has plans that someday it would be used to help us identify bias in our own conversations, designs and perspectives.

  Picture you are working on for solving a problem and you think you have considered every angle of the issue. Just to be certain, turn to the AI system and ask it to debate the idea with you.

  Within minutes the AI responds with counterpoints to your hypothesis. It offers points that can be specific to identifying potential biases you had not thought.

- **Design with Intention :** All of these solutions demonstrate much promise for eliminating the risks of embedding bias into the data models and interactions we create. But it is not enough to rely on data scientists, algorithms and AI itself to catch every bias within a system or to know what to do about it.

  Bias originates in humans. If we really want to control it, we have to learn to become aware of the bias in ourselves before creating machines. If we know the bias, then the machine would know how to deal with it for us.

  We need to find new practices that help us recognize biases and their causes and their effects in our daily lives and in the systems we build.

PRIVACY CONCERNS OF AI SYSTEMS

All online businesses use and deal with very large amount of data.

- This data is collected is on the basis of actions of their customers.
- This data is collected from various number of sources.
- It is gathered from customers' buying habits and their actions on their own online website and other websites, blogs, social media accounts and other sources. The data by these online companies is also gathered from third parties.

It is well known that consumers sacrifice their privacy when they use services that are freely available.

Think of Google and social media sites such as Facebook, WhatsApp. When you create an account on these sites, there is a contract (like ***I ACCEPT*** button) and sharing of various things like email id, photos, location etc.

This contract is a part and parcel of the terms and conditions that consumers or users agree to when they use services and sites like these.
Therefore, consumers know that the information they supply and the actions they do, will be used for) to target them with advertising.

AI can:

- do data-mining.
- arrange the data.
- draw conclusions from personal data about behaviour.

It is a Privacy Concern.

- A machine learning algorithm may dig out user's personal apps. It can supply the sensitive personal information to some Government agency.
- Personal fitness devices which many companies are providing to employees to gather data which could be used for insurance purposes.

All of this without human intervention.

The logical step for machine intelligence is to decide to whom the information should be supplied.

The risk is that many companies are collecting and processing a huge amount of user data in their AI-based system without their knowledge. It is a major privacy concern.

When you go to the Internet for searches, browsing websites or when you use mobile apps, you do not realize that you are giving away your data to them knowingly or unknowingly at a click of mouse.

With your personal information like name, age, email, contacts, videos or photo uploads, they also collect your browsing behaviour, likes and dislikes and even your mouse clicks. Reputed companies like Google and Facebook use this data to improve their services and do not sell this to anyone.

In fact, the intention of many companies is to collect user data sell this data for money to third parties.

There are various unreliable mobile apps whose main purpose is to collect data from the phone without user's permission.

Today, our smartphones contain very sensitive data like:

- chats
- personal images
- videos
- GPS location
- call history
- messages etc. and we do not even know that our data is getting stolen by these mobile apps.

Things Required for Privacy

- Principles of trustworthy AI
- Data confidentiality
- Data protection
- Transparency and fairness
- Non-discrimination
- Robustness
- Security of data processing
- Data protection and privacy laws

ETHICAL CONCERNS RELATED TO ADOPTION OF AI SYSTEMS

- **Job Loss and Wealth Inequality:** One of the primary concerns people have with AI is loss of jobs in future. As per reports, it is estimated that by the year 2030, about 800 million people will lose their jobs to AI-driven robots.

  One issue related to job loss is inequality of wealth. If robots were doing all the work in place of humans, the company will have not to pay wages, taxes, expenses and they will be doing the profit maximization. They will be getting richer and richer. This will create wealth inequality.
- **AI is Not Perfect:** Many thinkers are of the view that AI is not perfect. It makes mistakes. Sometimes the mistakes made by the AI systems are so dangerous that it can cost goodwill of the company and deteriorate its image.

Should AI Systems be Allowed to Take Sensitive Decisions?

A machine does what it learns to do. An incident was reported that computerized gun of a robot called Tallon was jammed and open fired uncontrollably after an explosion killing 9 people and wounding 14 more.

Drones have been in existence for the last few years. These can fire missiles. However, the actual command of firing the missile to be given by the defence authority but with drones playing more role in military, we need to further examine their role and how they are used.

What if the drones tend to behave inaccurately? Is it better to use AI to put human lives in danger?

Such areas and decisions are of high concerns.

- **Rogue AIs :** A super-intelligent centralized AI computer becomes self-aware and decides it does not want human control anymore.

  Experts say that existing AI technology is not capable of achieving this extremely dangerous feat of self-awareness.

  Think that AI has been tasked to study on a genetic virus and create a vaccine to neutralize it. After making lengthy calculations the AI formulated a solution to shoot the virus instead of making a vaccine.

- **Control of AI :**
  - Will AI surpass human beings?
  - What if the AI systems become smarter than human?
  - What if they try to control us?
  - Will computers make humans obsolete?

  Some experts believe that AI is a signal for the end of the human era. It is expected that by the year 2030, only the AI machines will be doing the tasks. This is the reason that advancement of AI is scary to many people.

- **How should We Treat AI?**

  Should robots be granted human rights?

  If robots are granted human rights, then how do we rank their social status?

  If AI systems surpasses human, the say of humans will be eliminated in various processes.

  Such thing also creates ethical concern in the humans.

ACCESS TO AI

Because hardware, software and staffing costs for AI can be expensive, many vendors are including AI components and services in their offerings.

With AI services, individuals and companies can experiment with AI for various business purposes and check sampling before making a purchase order.

Popular AI cloud offerings include:

- Amazon AI services
- IBM Watson Assistant
- Microsoft Cognitive Services
- Google AI services, etc.

ACCESS TO AI IN INDIAN SCENARIO

How AI can increase the reach of India's welfare schemes programmes to the public and make them efficient.

India has geared up for a brighter future powered by its 'AI for All' mission.

A study shows that AI could boost India's annual growth rate by 1.3 percentage points by 2035.

Let us see how AI can transform critical areas of public spending.

India is running a host of socially beneficial programs. Most of such programs aim to reach the millions of people who live in remote areas and a huge amount of funds is being spent every year on these programs.

The Government of India is ensuring that services reach all 1.3 billion citizens, including those residing in remote regions. It is a daunting task. AI-powered systems can be helpful in transforming the reach and effectiveness of public welfare programs.

Despite increased investment, India's public healthcare system has struggled to cope with the needs due to one or more of the following reasons:

- Growing population
- Pressure on hospitals due to increase in number of patients
- Private healthcare is very costly
- Public health system is not well equipped
- Low number of doctors
- Low success ratio in diagnosis

Technology might have the answer to this complex problem.

For Example:

An AI-powered system that collects and combines data on symptoms and suggests treatment based on similar cases will make the diagnostic process far more accurate and faster in public hospitals.

Such an AI system can be quickly scaled up to cover major urban centres and remote areas, which lack adequate medical infrastructure.

Health schemes can be benefitted AI for:

- Allocation of resources
- Geographic coverage
- Checking health records and applicants, claim patterns and trends, ensuring the scheme reaches those who need it the most.

AI technologies can help in mid-day meal scheme.

- Machine learning technology and supply chain planning could forecast inventory.

- Process automation technology can help in ensuring the right amount of high-quality food reaches schools on time and to the children. Automatic record of the meal given to a child on a particular day would be maintained by the machines.

  Machines would decide as to which food item is to be given to the children on a particular day of the week. Machines would also maintain the health records of the children and suggest the types of energy contents even for home food.

India is Facing Water Shortage Problem.

AI-powered smart water management systems are the solution for resolving this problem. These systems are called digital flowmeters. These systems track, measure and optimize water consumption in real time.

In Surat, such flowmeters have helped the Municipal Corporation do a more effective job of monitoring water consumption at 500 textile mills and make smarter decisions on water distribution.

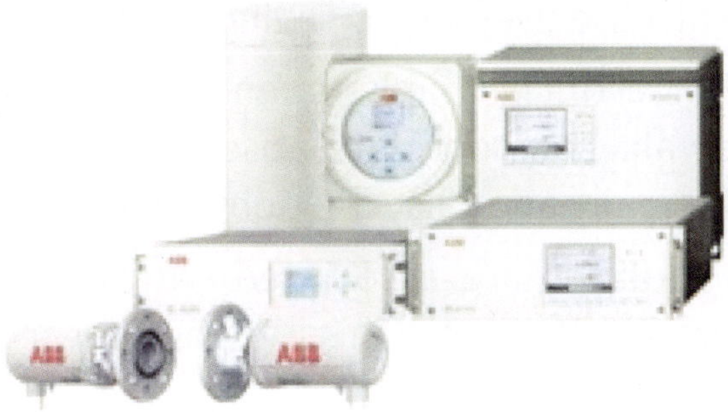

AI-powered systems can help the Government to make public spending to reach the targets in efficient way. AI has vast potential but it is yet to be explored in India. The Government and private organizations have to work together to overcome existing challenges such as lack of awareness in public and users and lack of effective privacy and security regulations.

Indian Government is releasing more funds for research, training and skill development in AI, digital manufacturing and robotics.

NITI Aayog has started working with major companies to work on various aspects of AI and increase awareness in areas like advanced manufacturing powered by AI and robotics.

Over time, India will be able to close the gap between data and action and pave the way to become one of the major technological-superpowers.

ADVANTAGES OF ARTIFICIAL INTELLIGENCE

Artificial Intelligence is complex in nature. It uses a mixture of Computer Science, Mathematics, Linguistics and other complex sciences. Complex programming helps these machines replicate the abilities of human beings.

Error Reduction

Artificial intelligence helps us in reducing errors and to reach accuracy with a greater degree of precision. It is applied in various studies such as space exploration, mining etc.

Intelligent robots are fed with the information and are sent to explore space. Since they are machines with metal bodies, they are more resistant and have a greater ability to bear the space and hostile atmosphere.

They are created in such a way that they cannot be modified or get disfigured in a hostile environment.

Difficult Exploration

Artificial intelligence and the science of robotics can be put to use in mining and fuel exploration. These complex machines can explore the ocean floor and overcome the human limitations.

Due to their programming, robots can perform more laborious and hard work with greater responsibility. Moreover, the robots do not wear out easily.

Digital Assistants

Highly advanced organizations use digital assistants that can actually interact with the users, thus saving the need for human resources.

For artificial thinkers, emotions and emotional thinking is not a distraction at all. The complete absence of the emotional side, makes the robots think logically and take the right decisions.

Emotions are associated with moods and feelings that can cloud your judgement and affect efficiency. This is completely ruled out in the case of machine intelligence.

Repetitive Jobs

Repetitive jobs can be carried out easily with the help of machine intelligence. Machines think faster and can be put to multi-tasking. Machine intelligence can be used effectively to carry out dangerous tasks.

When we play a computer game or run a computer-controlled robot, we are actually interacting with artificial intelligence. In the game, we are playing and the computer is our opponent. The machine intelligence plans the game movement on the basis of our movements. We can consider gaming to be the most common use of the of artificial intelligence.

Medical Applications

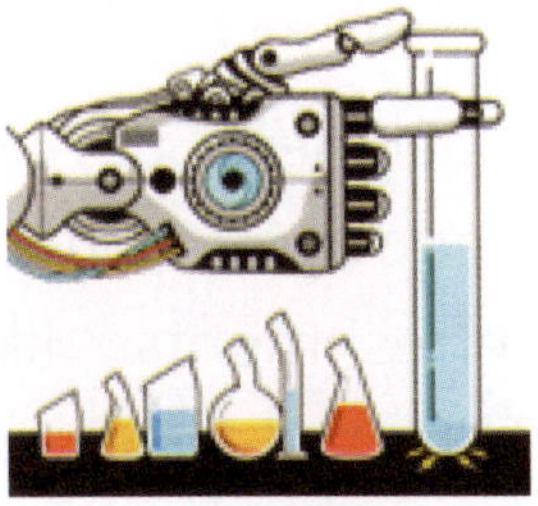

In the medical field, we find the wide application of AI. Doctors assess the patients and their health risks with the help of artificial intelligence. It educates the doctors about the side effects of various medicines.

Biometrics

AI and biometrics can work together to develop effective and reliable security systems. The combination of AI and biometrics helps in developing authentication systems. These systems can protect devices against cyber-attacks and prevent fraudulent activities.

AI and biometrics can work together in the following ways:

- **Keystroke Dynamics :** Keystroke dynamics is a method of identifying and authenticating people based on their keystrokes (typing) patterns. Keystroke dynamics can identify individuals with the help of their speed.
- **Facial Recognition :** Facial recognition is a popular feature in smartphones and on social networks like Facebook.
- Face recognition can be more effective with the help of machine learning. AI learns from millions of images and utilizes 3D biometrics to authenticate an individual's face. AI systems can also use predictive modelling to analyse the effects of aging on human faces.

- **Voice Recognition :** Several smart home devices such as Google Home and Amazon Alexa use voice and speech recognition for multiple tasks such as:

  - answering queries
  - ordering products
  - playing music etc.

  The implementation of AI in voice recognition can train the biometric systems by using millions of voice samples. AI and voice recognition can evaluate a person's biometric voice signature by analysing his voice patterns such as speed, accent, tone and pitch.
- **Gait Detection :** Gait detection is a method that authenticates individuals on the basis they walk. Gait detection can be a viable authentication solution with the help of AI.

No Breaks

Machines do not require frequent breaks and refreshments like humans. They are programmed for long hours and can continuously perform without getting tired or bored.

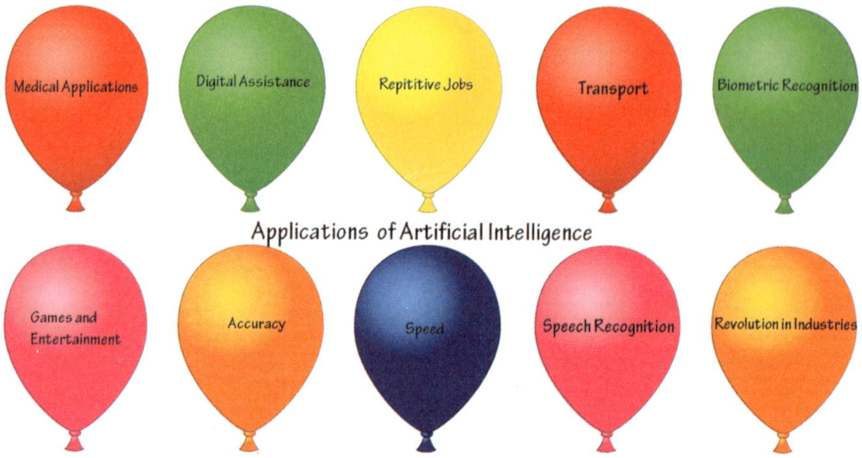

DISADVANTAGES OF ARTIFICIAL INTELLIGENCE

High Cost

Creation of artificial intelligence requires high costs of installation of machines. Repair and maintenance of these AI machines requires huge costs.

AI systems have software programs which need frequent upgradation to cater to the needs of the changing environment. In case of severe breakdowns, the procedure to recover lost codes and restoring the system might require huge time and cost.

Not a Replacement of Human

Intelligence is a gift of nature. Machines do not have any emotions or moral values. They perform on the basis of their programmed chips and cannot make the judgement of right or wrong. They cannot take decisions if they encounter a situation unfamiliar to them. They either perform incorrectly in such situations.

No Care and Concerns

Care or concerns are not present in the machine intelligence. There is no sense of belongingness or togetherness in it. Artificial Intelligence is unable to distinguish between a hardworking and an inefficient individual.

No Original Creativity

While AI can help you design and create, but it has no match to the power of thinking that the human brain has or even the originality of a creative mind.

Human beings are highly sensitive and emotional intellectuals. They see, hear, think and feel. Their thoughts are guided by the feelings and this feature lacks in the AI machines. The abilities of the human brain cannot be replicated and replaced with the machines.

Unemployment

Replacement of persons with machines can lead to large-scale unemployment. Unemployment is a socially undesirable phenomenon. People without jobs can use their creative minds in a destructive manner.

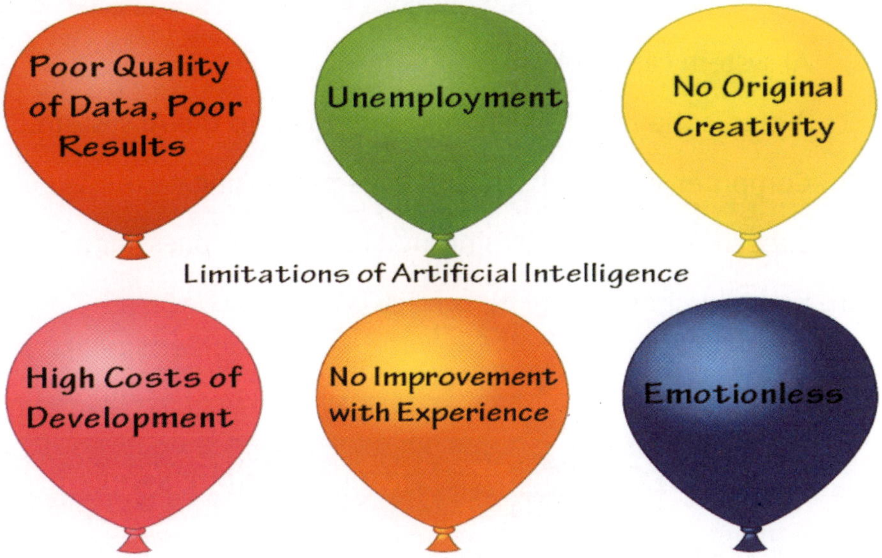

People can be highly dependent on the machines if there is excessive use of artificial intelligence. They may lose their creative power and will become lazy.

Artificial intelligence in wrong hands is a serious threat to the mankind in general. It may lead to mass destruction. There is a constant fear of machines superseding the humans.

EXERCISE

Performance Assessment, Review and Analysis

Fill in the Blanks with Given Hints

1. If a machine gives wrong results on genders, it is called a ________________.
2. Bias in AI occurs due to ________________.
3. AI systems give better results with ________________ large amount of data.
4. AI brings ________________ .

HINTS

Large, Bias, Automation, Data

Write T for True and F for False

1. AI system can work without datasets.
2. A bias is the result of bad datasets given to the AI system.
3. Computer Vision is used for image processing.
4. Speech recognition uses natural language processing.
5. In implementation of AI, privacy is not any concern.

Multiple Choice Questions

Tick the best alternatives.

1. An AI system shows the societal differences. It is a (an) ____________ .
   (a) Ethics (b) Bias
   (c) Both ethics and bias (d) None of these
2. AI cannot be used in ____________ .
   (a) Railways (b) Digital Programs
   (c) Defence system (d) None of these
3. AI can ____________ .
   (a) Increase the number of jobs
   (b) Decrease the number of jobs
   (c) Mixed effect
   (d) None of the above
4. A bias in an AI system can creep in due to ____________ .
   (a) Bad behaviour of the user with the machine
   (b) Intelligent behaviour of the user with the machine
   (c) Bad dataset given to the machine
   (d) Good dataset given to the machine

Competency Based Question

1. Nitika purchased some grocery items first time from an online grocery website. Since, mobile number was compulsory for purchase, she had to give her mobile number on a form on the website. She had a good experience of shopping from that grocery website, but the website started to send SMS and WhatsApp messages on her mobile phone relating to advertisements, product recommendations and so on. This is an issue of.

   (a) Lack of knowledge
   (b) Lack of interest
   (c) Gender bias
   (d) Data privacy

Answer the Following Questions

1. What is AI ethics?

2. What is the meaning of bias in AI system?

3. What is the impact of AI on jobs?

4. Write any two biases in artificial intelligence.

5. Write any two ethical issues related with the use of AI.

6. Write any two ethics to be followed while using artificial intelligence.

7. What are the benefits of artificial intelligence?

8. What are the limitations of artificial intelligence?

LAB ACTIVITY

For Students

Make a presentation on advantages and disadvantages in Artificial Intelligence.

Discuss:

- Bias in AI
- Ethics in AI

For Teachers

- Ethics is an important aspect of dealing with AI systems. With your experience you can tell various ethical issues involved in the use of AI technology in various fields. Give the students some suitable examples to create their interest in theoretical aspects of the AI ethics.
- Balloon Debate

  Divide the students divide in teams of 3 and 2 teams are given same theme. One team goes in affirmation to AI for their section while the other one goes against it.

  They have to come up with their points as to why AI is beneficial/ harmful for the society.

6

LOOPS IN PYTHON

Introduction

There may be a situation when we need to execute a block of code several number of times and is often referred to as a loop.

A loop is a way of repeating lines of code more than once. The block of code contained within the loop will be executed again and again until the condition required by the loop is met.

One of the things computers are often used for is the automation of repetitive tasks. Repeating identical or similar tasks without making errors is something that computers do well and people do poorly.

Let us study about loops which help us in repetitive tasks.

Learning Outcomes

- To understand and build the concept of looping. To solve day-to-day problems through programming.

Coverage:

The while loop, The for loop, Infinite loops, Nested loops, The else suite, The break statement, The continue statement

ITERATION STATEMENTS

Iterative statements are used to execute a part of the program repeatedly as long as a given condition is True.

When these statements are compound statements, they are executed in order except when either the break statement or the continue statement is encountered.

Selection	Iteration
In selection, a single statement or set of statements is either executed or skipped depending upon the test condition.	In Iteration, a single statement or set of statements is executed repeatedly till a condition is true.
Execution of a selected set of statements is maximum one.	Execution of a selected set of statements can be more than once.

LOOPS

Loop construct is a repetitive control structure in nature. Sometimes we require a set of statements to be executed number of times by changing the values of one or more variables each time to obtain a different result. This type of program execution is called *Looping*.

Need of Loops

Loops are the heart of programming. To write an efficient program, loops are required.

Imagine that you have to write a program which performs a repetitive task such as counting from 1 to 100. Coding 100 lines to do this task would be very cumbersome. Loops can help you.

Loops are specifically designed to perform repetitive tasks with one set of code. Loops save a lot of time. Loops are important for programming due to the following reasons:

- Loops make the program code shorter. For known or unknown number of iterations, they are used in the programs to execute the part of the program up to a fixed number of times or till a condition is met.
- Nested loops are used for calculations in matrices and arrays. They can be used for sorting of array elements, prepare number tables, searching an element, etc.
- Loops can be used for recursion process. Methods can be used through loops and need of calling them again and again is avoided.
- Loops can be used for calculations.

Python has very flexible two looping mechanisms for iterations. You can use any one of the following loops:

- for Loop
- while Loop

In addition to these two loops, there is another form of for loop *i.e.* nested for loop.

Without loops good programming cannot be thought. Loops are the basis of simple to complex programming.

FOR LOOP IN PYTHON

A for loop is used for iterating a sequence (that is either a list, a tuple, a dictionary, a set or a string) or part of a program.

With the for loop, we can execute a set of statements, once for each item in a list, tuple, set, etc.

The basic structure of the for loop is:

```
for item_in_sequence:
    execute expression
```

where:

- for starts a for loop.
- item is an individual item during each iteration(you can say the item is a variable).
- If a sequence contains an expression list, it is evaluated first.
- the first item in the sequence is assigned to the iterating variable item.
- in separates each item from the other(s).
- sequence is what we want to iterate over.
- a colon: gives the instruction to execute the body of code that follows.
- A new line.

A level of indentation. 4 spaces before writing the body of the loop, otherwise we get an IndentationError.

The body with the actions that need to be taken and repeated

For Example:

Print something to the console. It goes where the execute expression line is.

Flowchart of For Loop

Processing of For Loop

- The loop variable is assigned the first value in the sequence.
- All the statements in the body of for loop are executed with assigned value of loop variable. (first value in start).
- Once all the statements of the body of for loop are executed after assigning the first value, the next value is assigned to the loop variable.
- This process continues till all the values are assigned to the loop variable.

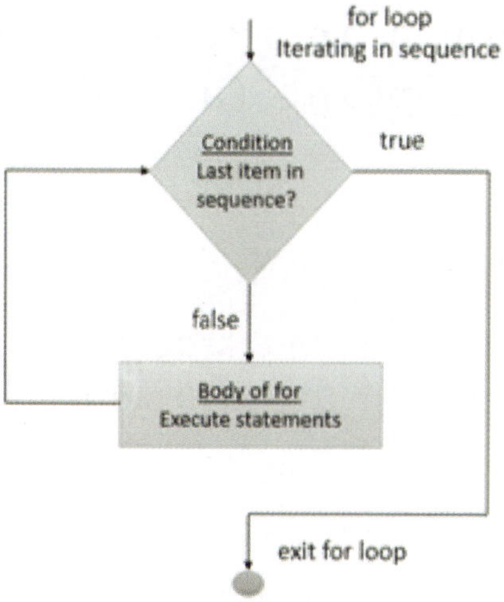

The for loop is better when you are counting something. It you are doing something an indefinite number of times, while loop may be the better choice.

For Example:

```
for a in [1, 2, 3, 4]:
    print (a)
    print (a + a)
```

```
1
2
2
4
3
6
4
8
```

Look at the given program: In this program, in the first statement, the loop variable is a. It will be assigned each value of the list one by one. First it will get 1, then 2 and so on.

After for statement, the body of the loop starts. All statements in the body of the loop will be executed for each value of loop variable a.

For Example:

1.

```
for chr in "SCHOOL":
    print(chr)

S
C
H
O
O
L
```

In the above loop, the variable chr is given the value of characters of string SCHOOL one by one. It should be noted that strings are also iterable objects in Python.

2. Print each colour in a colour list:

```
colour = ["red", "green", "blue"]
for x in colour:
    print(x)
```

```
red
green
blue
```

3.

```
for a in [3, 4, 5] :
    print (a * a)
```

```
9
16
25
```

range( ) Function

We can generate a sequence of numbers using range() function. range(10) will generate numbers from 0 to 9 (10 numbers).

We can also define the start, stop and step size as range(start, stop, step size).

- The step size defaults to 1 (if you do not provide).

This function does not store all the values in memory. It remembers the start, stop, step size and generates the next number on the go.

To force this function to output all the items, we can use the function list( ).

The following example will clarify this.

```
print(range(10))
print(list(range(10)))
print(list(range(2, 8)))
print(list(range(2, 20, 3)))

range(0, 10)
[0, 1, 2, 3, 4, 5, 6, 7, 8, 9]
[2, 3, 4, 5, 6, 7]
[2, 5, 8, 11, 14, 17]
```

We can use the range( ) function in for loops to iterate through a sequence of numbers. It can be combined with the len( ) function to iterate though a sequence using indexing.

PROGRAMS ON FOR LOOP

1. Program to print the multiplication table of a number.

```
num = 12
for i in range(1, 11):
   print(num, 'x', i, '=', num * i)
```

```
12 x 1 = 12
12 x 2 = 24
12 x 3 = 36
12 x 4 = 48
12 x 5 = 60
12 x 6 = 72
12 x 7 = 84
12 x 8 = 96
12 x 9 = 108
12 x 10 = 120
```

2. Program to find the sum and average of n numbers.

```
n = input("Enter numbers::")
n = int(n)
average = 0
sum = 0
for num in range(0, n+1,1):
    sum = sum + num
print("Sum of first ", n, "numbers is:: ", sum )
```

```
Enter numbers::4
Sum of first  4 numbers is::  10
```

3. Program to find the sum and average of the numbers in a given list.

```
sum = 0
list = [1, 2, 3, 4, 5, 6,7, 8]
for num in list:
    sum = sum + num
average  = sum / len(list)
print ("Sum of list element is : ", sum)
print ("Average of list element is : ", average )
```

```
Sum of list element is :  36
Average of list element is :  4.5
```

4. Program to find the factorial of a number.

```
num = int(input("Enter a number: "))
factorial = 1
if num < 0:
   print(" Invalid input.")
elif num == 0:
   print("The factorial of 0 is 1")
else:
   for i in range(1, num + 1):
       factorial = factorial * i
   print("Factorial of ", num," is ", factorial)
```

```
Enter a number: 5
Factorial of  5  is  120
```

Use of Else Statement

Python allows the else keyword both with the for and while loops.

The else block appears after the body of the loop. The statements in the else block will be executed after all iterations are completed. The program exits the loop only after the else block is executed.

- If the else statement is used with a for loop, the else statement is executed when the loop has exhausted iterating the list.
- If the else statement is used with a while loop, the else statement is executed when the condition becomes false.

The else block just after *for/while* is executed only when the loop is not terminated by a break statement.

Use of Else in For Loop

A for loop can have an optional else block as well. The else part is executed if the items in the sequence used in for loop exhausts.

The break statement can be used to stop a for loop. In such case, the else part is ignored. Hence, a else part of a for loop runs if no break occurs.

For Example:

```
num = [0, 1, 2, 4]
for i in num:
    print(i)
else:
    print("All items completed.  Nothing left now.")
```

Here, the for loop prints items of the list until the loop exhausts. When the for loop exhausts, it executes the block of code in the else and prints :

```
0
1
2
4
All items completed.  Nothing left now.
```

For Example:

```
for x in range(5):
  print(x)
else:
  print("I have printed 0 to 5.")

0
1
2
3
4
I have printed 0 to 5.
```

The above code prints all the numbers from 0 to 4 and also prints a message when the loop has finished.

WHILE LOOP IN PYTHON

The while loop is used to iterate over a block of code repeatedly until a given condition returns false. The main difference in while and for loop is that while loop is used when we are not certain of the number of times the loop requires execution, whereas, for loop is used when the number of iterations (how many times the loop will run) is known.

Syntax:

```
while condition:
    body_of_while
```

In while loop, condition is checked first. The body of the loop is entered only if the condition evaluates to True. After first iteration, the test expression is checked again. This process continues until the condition evaluates to False.

Python interprets any non-zero value as True. None and 0 are interpreted as False.

Flowchart for While Loop

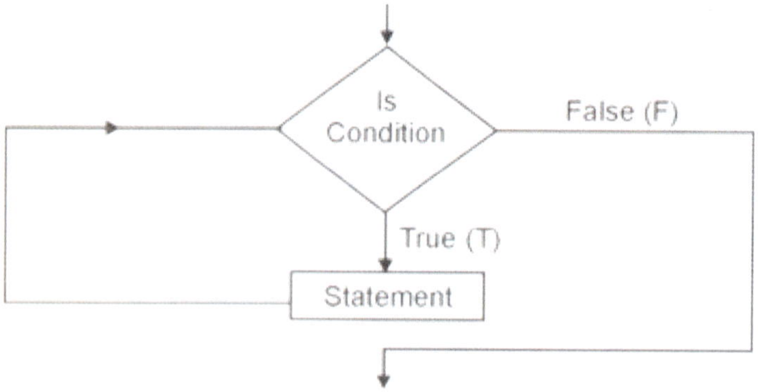

Processing of While Loop

- First the given condition is checked, if the condition returns false, the loop is terminated and the control jumps to the next statement in the program after the loop.
- If the condition returns true, the set of statements inside loop are executed and then the control jumps to the beginning of the loop for next iteration.

These two steps happen repeatedly as long as the condition specified in the while loop remains true.

For Example:

```
num = 1
while num < 10:
    print(num)
    num = num + 3
```

```
1
4
7
```

In the above example, value of variable num is being printed in a loop. The loop has an increment operation where we are increasing the value of num by 3.

The while loop must have an increment or decrement operation, else the loop will run indefinitely.

> **Note**
>
> Both the for and while loops are entry-controlled loops in Python.
>
> An entry-controlled loop checks the condition at the time of entering into the body of loop. Only if the condition is true, the program control enters the body of the loop.

Infinite While Loop

A loop becomes infinite loop if a condition remains always True. Since the condition is always True, the loop never stops. Such a loop is called an infinite loop.

For Example :

```
while True:
    print("PYTHON")
```

This will print the word PYTHON indefinitely because the condition will always be true.

For Example :

```
num = 1
while num < 2:
   print(num)
```

This will print 1 indefinitely because inside loop, the value of num is not being updated, therefore, the value of num will always remain 1 and the condition num < 2 will always return true.

Nested While Loop

When a while loop is present inside another while loop then it is called nested while loop.

For Example :

```
i = 1
j = 5
while i < 4:
    while j < 10:
        print(i, "<", j)
        j = j + 1
        i = i + 1
```

```
1 < 5
2 < 6
3 < 7
4 < 8
5 < 9
```

The While Loop with Else

We can have an else clause with the while loop. The else statement is optional. It executes only after the loop finished execution.

For Example :

```
num = 20
while num > 10:
   print(num)
   num = num - 1
else:
   print("Loop Completed")
```

```
20
19
18
17
16
15
14
13
12
11
Loop Completed
```

JUMP STATEMENTS

Jump statements in Python are used to alter the flow of a loop like skippin a part of a loop or terminate a loop.

Types of Jump statements in Python are:

1. break
2. continue
3. pass

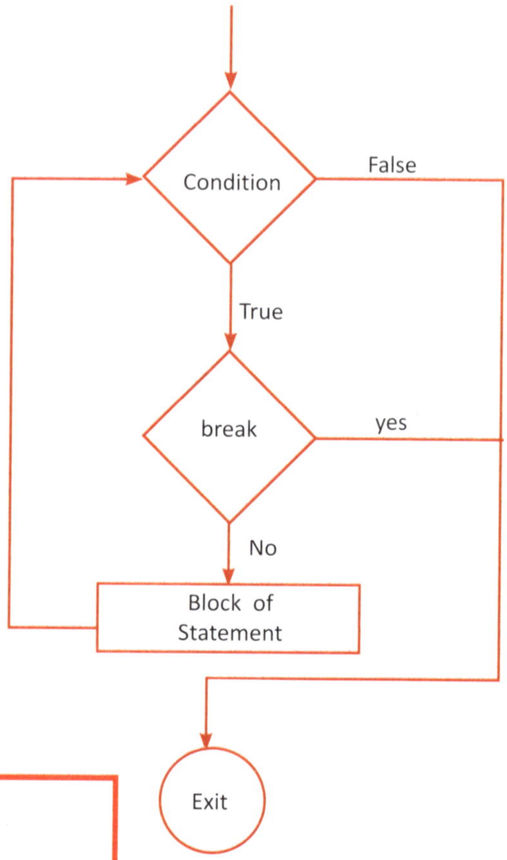

The break Statement

The break statement is used to exit a for or a while loop. The purpose of this statement is to end the execution of the loop (for or while) immediately and the program control goes to the statement after the last statement of the loop. If there is an optional else statement in while or for loop it skips the optional clause also.

Syntax:

```
while (expression1):
    statement_1
    statement_2
    .......
    if expression2:
        break
    for variable_name in sequence:
        statement_1
        statement_2
        if expression3:
            break
```

Break in For Loop

In the following example for loop breaks when the count value is 5. The print statement after the for loop displays the sum of first 5 elements of the tuple numbers.

```
numbers = (1, 2, 3, 4, 5, 6, 7, 8, 9) # Declaring the tuple
num_sum = 0
count = 0
for x in numbers:
    num_sum = num_sum + x
    count = count + 1
    if count == 5:
        break
print("Sum of first ",count,"integers is: ", num_sum)
```

```
Sum of first  5 integers is:  15
```

Break in While Loop

In the following example while loop breaks when the count value is 5. The print statement after the while loop displays the value of num_sum (*i.e.* 0+1+2+3+4).

```
num_sum = 0
count = 0
while(count < 10):
    num_sum = num_sum + count
    count = count + 1
    if count == 5:
        break
print("Sum of first ",count, "integers is: ", num_sum)
```

```
Sum of first  5 integers is:  10
```

The continue Statement

The continue statement is used in a while or for loop to take the control to the top of the loop without executing the rest statements inside the loop.

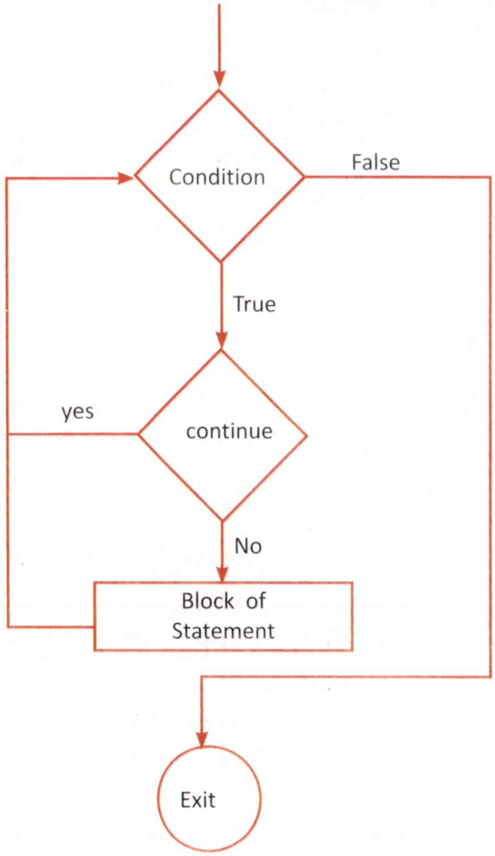

For Example :

```
for x in range(7):
    if (x == 3 or x==6):
        continue
    print(x)
```

```
0
1
2
4
5
```

In the above example, the for loop prints all the numbers from 0 to 6 except 0 and 6 as the continue statement returns the control of the loop to the top.

The distinction between break and continue is demonstrated in the following diagram:

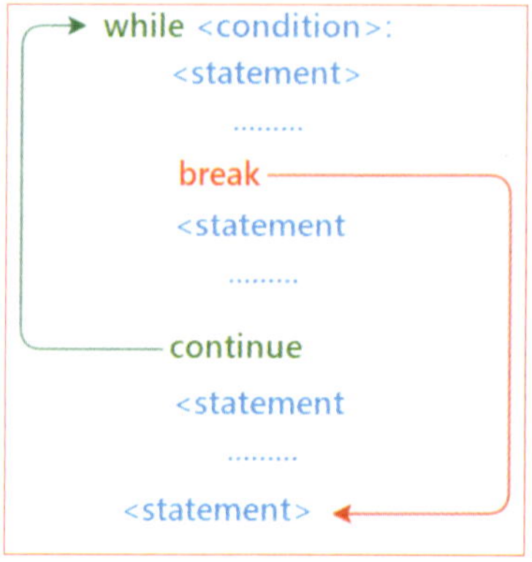

break and continue

The pass Statement

The pass statement does nothing. You can use the pass statement when you create a method that you do not want to implement yet but later on.

The pass statement makes a controller to pass by without executing any code.

For Example :

```
for i in 'aeiouAEIOU':
    if(i == 'a'):
        pass
    else:
        print(i)
```

```
e
i
o
u
A
E
I
O
U
```

NESTED LOOPS

Python programming language allows to use one loop inside another loop. Following section shows few examples to illustrate the concept.

Syntax:

The syntax of a nested for loop statement is as follows:

```
for iterating_var in sequence:
    for iterating_var in sequence:
        statement_1
        statement_2
        ...........
```

The syntax of a nested while loop statement is as follows:

```
while expression:
    while expression:
        statement_1
        statement_2
        ...........
```

You can put any type of loop inside of any other type of loop, *e.g.*, a for loop can be inside a while loop or vice versa.

For Example:

```
for i in range(1, 7):
    for j in range (1, i):
        print("*", end = ' ')
    print( )
```

```
*
* *
* * *
* * * *
* * * * *
```

The print( ) function in inner loop has end = ' ' which appends a space instead of default newline. Hence, the numbers will appear in one row.

Last print( ) will be executed at the end of inner for loop.

In the given program, there is an inner for loop between the body of outer for loop. The inner loop is executed for each value of i. The value of variable i takes values 1, 2, 3, 4 and 5. The inner loop is executed once for i = 1(according to the range (1, i), because for i = 1, there is just one element in the range(1, 1). Therefore, j iterates for one value *i.e.* 1.). When i = 2, j iterates for two values in the range (1, 2) and so on....).

It is to be noted that the value of outer loop variable will change only after the inner loop is finished (completed) or interrupted in some way.

For Example:

```
numlist = [1, 2, 3]
alphalist = ['Z', 'A']
for number in numlist:
    print(number)
    for letter in alphalist:
        print(letter)
```

```
1
Z
A
2
Z
A
3
Z
A
```

In the illustration, the program completes the first iteration of the outer loop by printing 1, which then triggers completion of the inner loop, printing Z, A. Once the inner loop has completed, the program returns to the top of the outer loop, prints 2, then again prints the inner loop with Z, A and so on.

For Example:

The following program uses a nested for loop to find the prime numbers from 2 to 50.

```
i = 2
while(i < 50):
   j = 2
   while(j <=  (i / j)):
      if not(i % j):
        break
      j = j + 1
   if (j > i / j):
        print(" ", i)
   i = i + 1
print("WORK DONE.")
```

```
2
3
5
7
11
13
17
19
23
29
31
37
41
43
47
WORK DONE.
```

WORKED OUT PROGRAMS IN PYTHON

1. Program to print the following pattern.

1
11
111
1111
11111
111111

```
n =1
for a in range(6):
    print (n)
    n = n * 10 + 1
```

2. Program to print the following pattern.

1
2 2
3 3 3
4 4 4 4
5 5 5 5 5

```
for num in range(6):
    for i in range(num):
        print(num, end = ' ')
    print(' ')
```

3. Program to print the following pattern.

1
13
135
1357

```
for a in range(3, 10, 2):
    for b in range(1, a, 2):
        print(b, end = ' ')
    print( )
```

4. Program to print the following pattern.

A
AB
ABC
ABCD
ABCDE
ABCDEF

```
ascii_value = 65
for i in range(6):
    for j in range(i + 1):
        alphabet = chr(ascii_value)
        print(alphabet, end = ' ')
    ascii_value += 1
    print( )
```

5. Program to calculate sum of odd numbers from 1 to n using for loop.

```
n = int(input("Enter the n Value : "))
sumodd = 0
print("Odd numbers are:")
for number in range(1, n + 1):
    if(number % 2 != 0):
        print("{0}".format(number))
        sumodd = sumodd + number
print("The Sum of Odd Numbers from 1 to {0} = {1}".format(number, sumodd))

Enter the n Value : 5
Odd numbers are:
1
3
5
The Sum of Odd Numbers from 1 to 5 = 9
```

6. Program to calculate sum of even numbers from 1 to n using for loop.

```
n = int(input("Enter the n Value: "))
sumeven = 0
print("Even numbers are:")
for number in range(1, n):
    if(number % 2 == 0):
        print("{0}".format(number))
        sumeven = sumeven + number
print("The Sum of Even Numbers from 1 to {0} = {1}".format(number, sumeven))

Enter the n Value: 5
Even numbers are:
2
4
The Sum of Even Numbers from 1 to 4 = 6
```

7. Program to calculate sum of odd numbers from 1 to n using while loop.

```
n = int(input("Enter the value: "))
sumodd = 0
number = 1
print("Odd numbers are:")
while number <= n:
    if(number % 2 != 0):
        print("{0}".format(number))
        sumodd = sumodd + number
    number = number + 1
print("The Sum of Odd Numbers from 1 to {0} = {1}".format(n, sumodd))

Enter the value: 10
Odd numbers are:
1
3
5
7
9
The Sum of Odd Numbers from 1 to 10 = 25
```

8. Program to calculate sum of odd numbers from 1 to n using while loop.

```
n = int(input("Enter the value: "))
sumeven = 0
number = 1
print("Even numbers are:")
while number <= n:
    if(number % 2 == 0):
        print("{0}".format(number))
        sumeven = sumeven + number
    number = number + 1
print("The Sum of Even Numbers from 1 to {0} = {1}".format(n, sumeven))

Enter the value: 10
Even numbers are:
2
4
6
8
10
The Sum of Even Numbers from 1 to 10 = 30
```

EXERCISE

Performance Assessment, Review and Analysis

Fill in the Blanks with Given Hints

1. The for loop is used for ______________________ .
2. The ______________________ loop is used for fixed number of iterations.
3. The for loop is called ______________________ controlled loop.
4. There are ______________________ types of loops in Python.
5. ______________________ is a jump statement.
6. The for loop works on ______________________ and iteration.

HINTS

for, range, entry, two, goto, iteration

Write T for True and F for False

1. The for loop is an iterative control statement. [ ]
2. The while loop is a decision-making statement. [ ]
3. The for loop is used when the number of iterations is not known. [ ]

4. The while loop is used when the number of iterations is known. [ ]
5. The break and continue are the jump statements. [ ]

Multiple Choice Questions

Tick ✓ the best alternatives.

1. Which of the following is a looping statement ?
   (a) for [ ] (b) break [ ]
   (c) if [ ] (d) None of these [ ]
2. The while loop is a/an ____________________ .
   (a) entry-controlled loop [ ] (b) exit-controlled loop [ ]
   (c) conditional [ ] (d) None of these [ ]
3. The while is a/an ____________________ .
   (a) continue clause [ ] (b) repetitive control structure [ ]
   (c) break construct [ ] (d) None of these [ ]
4. The break statement is used to ____________________ .
   (a) exit a for loop [ ] (b) exit a while loop [ ]
   (c) Both (a) and (b) [ ] (d) None of these [ ]
5. The for loop works on ____________________ .
   (a) range [ ] (b) iteration [ ]
   (c) Both of these [ ] (d) None of these [ ]
6. Which of the following loops can check the condition?
   (a) for loop [ ] (b) while loop [ ]
   (c) if conditional [ ] (d) elif conditional [ ]
7. To break an infinite loop which of the following statement is used?
   (a) continue [ ] (b) break [ ]
   (c) exit [ ] (d) None of these [ ]
8. Which of the following is not a loop in Python?
   (a) for [ ] (b) while [ ]
   (c) do while [ ] (d) None of these [ ]

9. Which of the following keywords can be used to work on a particular range?

(a) while (b) do while

(c) break (d) for

10. A loop block in starts with a ______________________ .

(a) ; (semicolon) (b) , (comma)

(c) # (hash) (d) : (colon)

11. Which of the following is not a valid keyword of Python associated with loops?

(a) continue (b) stop

(c) range (d) break

12. ______________________ in Python can be termed as a counter-controlled loop.

(a) while (b) for

(c) Both (a) and (b) (d) None of these

13. What is another name for 'iteration'?

(a) selection (b) assignment

(c) sequencing (d) repetition

14. Which of the following will run as an infinite loop?

(a) while(infinte): (b) while(1):

(c) while(not 1): (d) while(!1)

15. How many times will this loop run?

```
while(1==2):
    pass
```

(a) 0 (b) 1

(c) Infinite (d) 4

16. Which of the following call to range( ) in Python will not output anything?

(a) range(-6, -1) (b) range(-1, -6, -1)

(c) range(-6) (d) All of these

17. Which of the following is not a valid jump statement in Python?

(a) break (b) goto

(c) call (d) continue

18. Statement 1. The while statement is used as a looping statement.

Statement 2. The for statement is also used as a looping statement.

Statement 3. Both the while and loop statements are the same.

(a) All the three statements are true

(b) All the three statements are false

(c) Statements 1 and 2 are true, but statement 3 is false

(d) Statement 1 and 3 are true but statement 3 is false

19. Statement 1. The for loop is used when we know the number of iterations in advances.

Statement 2. The while loop is used when we do not know how many iterations must occur in a loop.

(a) both the statements are true

(b) both the statements are false

(c) Statement 1 is true but Statement 2 is false

(d) Statement 1 is false but Statement 2 is true

Programming Based Questions

1. Write a Python program to check whether a number is even or odd.
2. Write a Python program to check whether a number is perfect or not.
3. Write a for loop which displays the numbers 30 to 1, *i.e.,* 30, 29, ____________1.
4. Write a for loop which displays the numbers 50 to 100.
5. Write a while loop which displays the numbers 1, 3, 5, ... 51.
6. Write a program to print the following pattern.

```
1
2 3 2
3 4 5 4 3
4 5 6 7 6 5 4
5 6 7 8 9 8 7 6 5
```

7. Write a program to print the following pattern.

```
54321
5432
543
54
5
```

8. Write a program to print the following pattern.

```
Z
Y Y
X X X
W W W W
V V V V V
U U U U U U
```

9. Write a program to find the sum of first 20 odd numbers and also their average using while loop.

Answer the Following Questions

1. What is iteration?

2. What is a loop?

3. What are the uses of loops in programming?

4. What are the types of loops in Python?

5. What is the use of while loop?

6. What is the difference between for and while loop?

7. What is the use of else statement with the for loop?

8. What is the use of else statement with the while loop?

9. What is the use of break statement?

10. What is the use of continue statement?

____

____

11. What is the use of pass statement in a program?

____

____

12. What is a nested loop?

____

____

13. What is an infinite loop?

____

____

LAB ACTIVITY

For Students

Prepare a practical notebook to cover the additional programs in Python on daily situations like:

- Mathematical tables
- Solutions of mathematical problems
- Designs and patterns

Discuss:

During the Lab session, discuss these questions in a group of 4 students.

- Iteration
- Looping
- for and while loops
- break statement
- continue statement

For Teachers

- Teacher may explain the topics with more and more examples to form the solid base for the students for programming in Python. The detailed coverage of topics with live examples can create interest of the students towards better programming.

Project Work

ARTIFICIAL INTELLIGENCE-BASED HOME AUTOMATION

Introduction

In this project, will control the appliances using the Speech Recognition technology. We are going to create a small set up of a bedroom in PictoBlox and control the appliance sprites using the voice commands.

Prerequisites

- A laptop or a computer with a camera
- The latest version of PictoBlox
- A high-speed Internet connection
- The software can be downloaded from the link:

https://thestempedia.com/product/ictoblox/download-pictoblox/ Scan code

Setting Up the Project

1. Open PictoBlox.
2. Click on Board and select evive.

   To work with the latest AI and ML extension:

   - Your computer needs to be connected to the Internet
   - You have to login into PictoBlox.

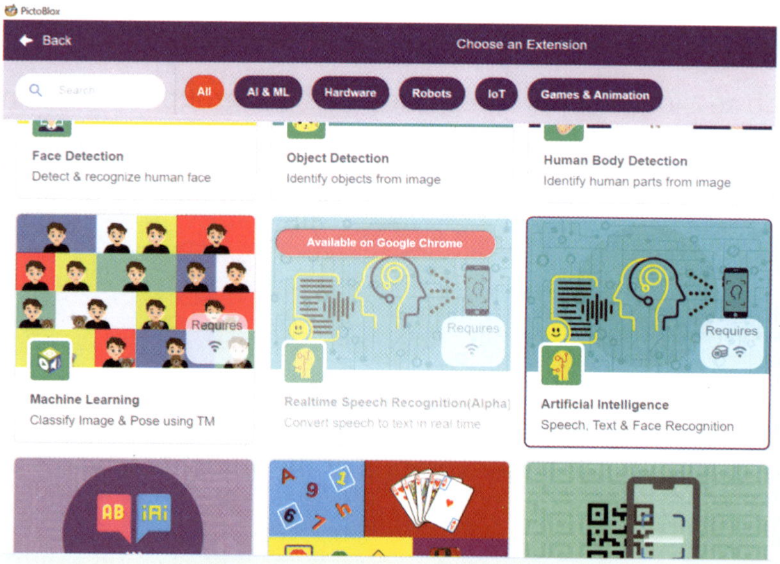

3. Click on the Add Extension button.
4. Select the Artificial Intelligence extension.
5. Add the Text to Speech extension. This extension lets you convert the Audio into a text message.
6. Click on the Add Extension button again and scroll down till you find the Text to Speech extension.

Setting Up the Bedroom in the PictoBlox

1. Once you have downloaded the script of your choice, go to PictoBlox.
2. Now set up the Stage by adding the Sprite and the Backdrop.
3. Choose the File option to open up the downloaded script.

   We will be controlling four sprites:

   - Fan, which we will turn ON and OFF
   - Lamp, which we will turn ON and OFF
   - The Music will play the Spiderman song on it.
   - Hazel will be our virtual AI assistant.

Scripts to Give Command to AI Assistant

Introducing Hazel

We will make our sprite Hazel to ask the person what can she do for him?

1. Place when flag clicked hat block from the Events palette.
2. Hazel is standing in the centre of the stage. We can shift her position to the left-hand side of the stage. Use go to x () y () block from the Motion palette and write -200 in x and 0 in the y.

3. Set the size of sprite to 200% of the original. Use the set size to () block from the Looks palette and write 200 in the space given.

4. To give voice to Hazel, place speak, place set voice to () block from the Text to Speech extension and choose tenor from the drop-down options.
5. Drag and drop say () for () seconds block from the Looks palette and write "Hello and Welcome! I am your Assistant".
6. Place a speak block and copy the above sentence into the white space given.
7. Drag and drop say () for () seconds block from the Looks palette and write "Hello and Welcome! I am your Assistant".

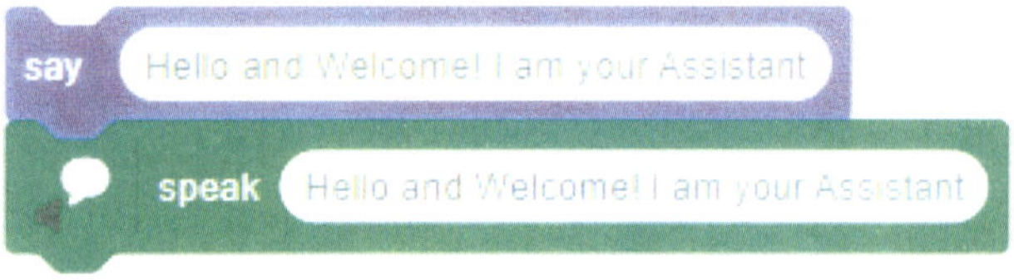

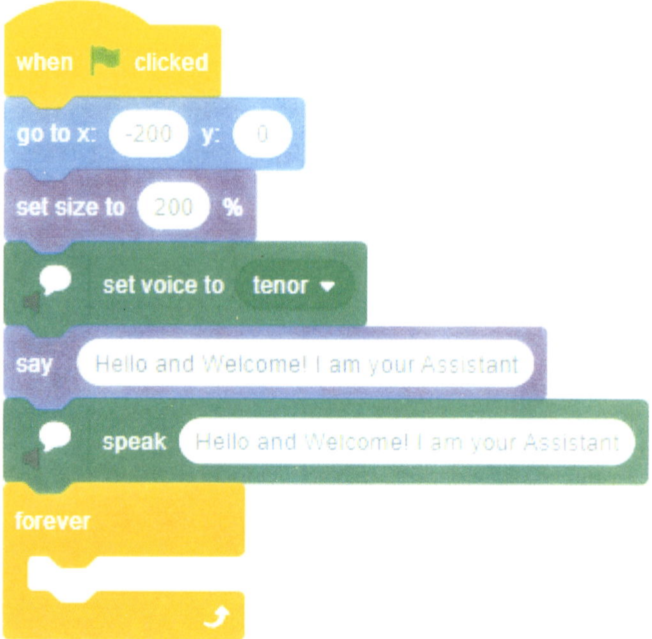

8. To make her say the text, place a speak block and copy the above sentence into the white space given.
9. Now, place a forever block to run the script continuously.

Asking for User Commands

1. Now, Hazel will ask the user what help she can do for them. Duplicate say and speak blocks and write "How can I help you?" in both of the spaces given.

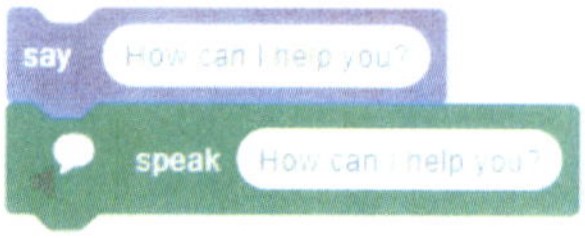

2. To recognize the speech from the user, thus, from the Artificial Intelligence drag and drop the recognize speech for () sec in () block and choose 2 from the first drop-down to keep how long do we recognize speech from the user.
3. Now, the speech is recognized but is not stored in the block, it is stored in the speech recognition result block.

Now, we will match the speech from the user to the text we have added thus, place an if-else block from the Controls palette.

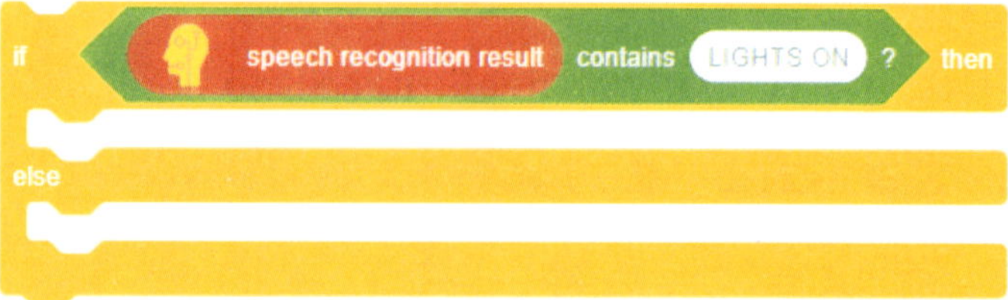

Now, to compare the recognized speech and the command, place a () contains () operator block from the Operators palette. This block is used to check whether the user has spoken the phrase written in the space.

Commands for Lights

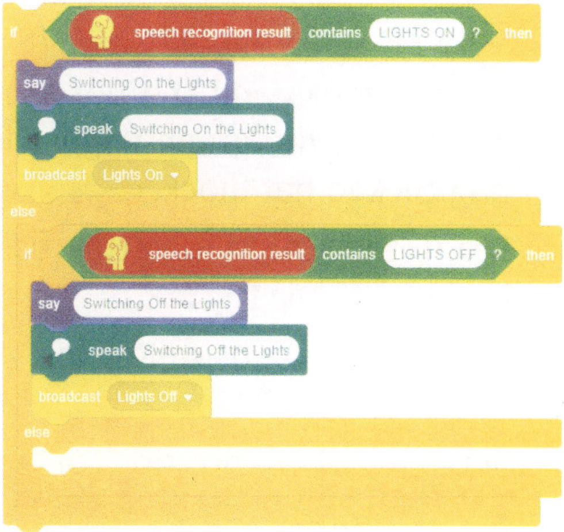

1. Place the speech recognition result in the first space. To turn the Lights ON, write "LIGHTS ON" in the second space of the *contains* block.
2. Make Hazel say "Switching On the Lights". place the say and the speak blocks below into if part.
3. To turn the light ON, place a broadcast block and write the new message as "Lights On".
4. To make the light Turn OFF, make a duplicate of the if-else block and place it into the else part.
5. Replace all the ONs with OFFs.

Commands for Fans

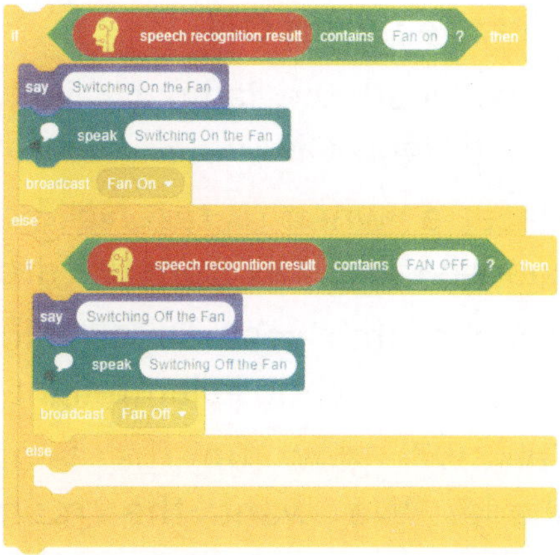

1. To make the Fan turn ON and OFF, replace the above nested if-else part and place it into the else part.
2. Into the duplicated else arm, replace all the light word with Fan.

Commands for Music

1. To turn the Music ON and OFF, make a duplicate of the last two if-else parts and place into the else part.
2. Replace Fan with Music.
3. If the commands spoken by the user do not match any of the above commands, then Hazel will say "Sorry, I do not know, Tell me again".

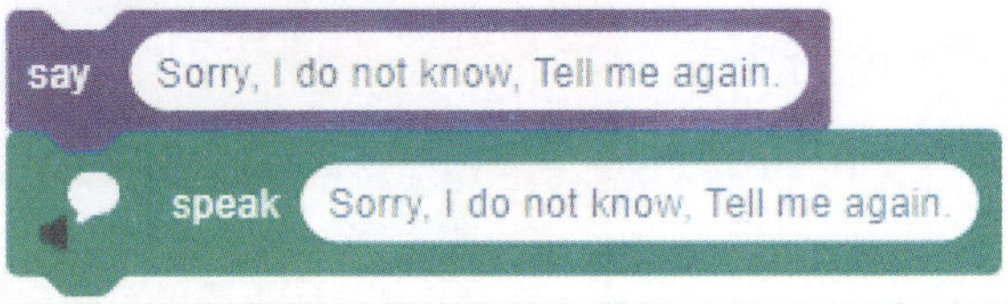

4. Place the say and the speak blocks for the same.

Now write the script to make each and every appliance work when the command is given.

Script for the Lights

1. Click on the lamp-light sprite.
2. Set the looks and the position of the lamp sprite as soon as the green flag is clicked. Place a when flag clicked hat block.
3. From the Looks palette, using the set size to block, set size to 40%.
4. Switch the costume to lamp-light-1
5. Set the initial position of go to x () y () block from the Motion palette and write -30 in x and 20 in the y.

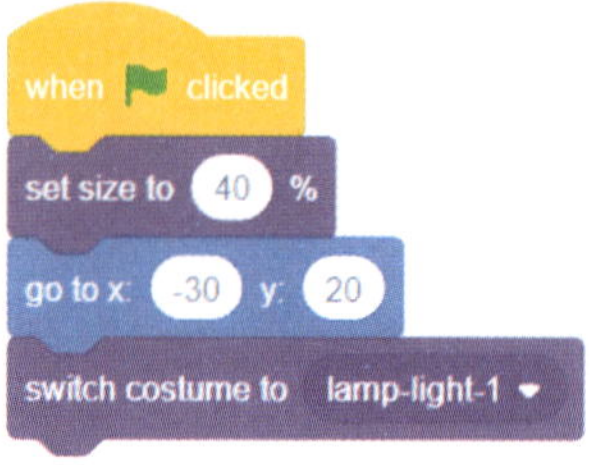

Turning the Lights ON

Now, we need the lamp to light up as soon as we command Lights ON.

1. Place a when I receive broadcast block and choose Lights ON from the drop-down.
2. Place switch costume to block from the Looks palette and choose lamp-light-2.
3. This will glow up the lamp shade. We want the room to lighten up as soon as the Lights are ON.

4. Go to the backdrop. To set the brightness of the room, place a when flag clicked hat block.
5. From the Looks palette, using the set brightness effect to block, set it to -10.
6. Now to lighten up the room. Place a when I receive broadcast block and choose "Lights On" from the drop-down.
7. In the set brightness effect to block set the brightness to 20.
8. Go back to the lamp sprite to write script for what happens when we turn the Lamp OFF.

Turning the Lights OFF

1. Duplicate these blocks and choose Lights OFF from the first drop-down and lamp-light-animation from here to stop making the lamp shade glow.
2. Finally, we need to turn the room dark as soon as we command Lights OFF.
3. Go to backdrop and make duplicate of these blocks.
4. Choose Lights OFF from the first drop-down and write -10 in here.

   Script for the lamp is complete.

Script for the Fan

1. To make the fan rotate go to the Fan sprite.
2. Place a when flag clicked hat block.
3. From the Looks palette, using the set size to block, set its size to 65%.
4. Switch the costume to fan.
5. Use go to x () y () block from the Motion palette and write 65 in x and 150 in the y.

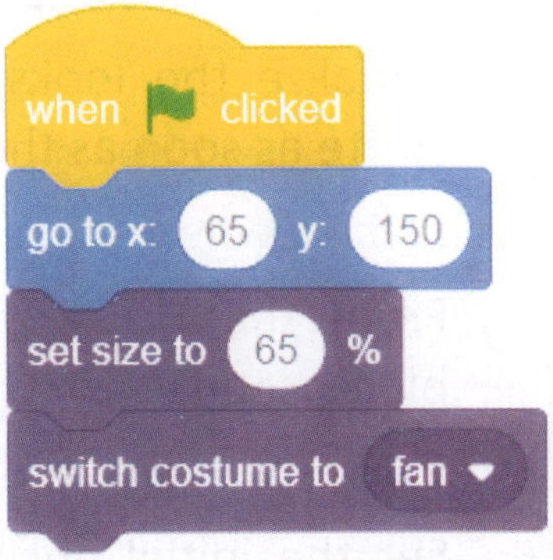

Turning the Fan ON

1. To make the lamp to light up as soon as we command Fan ON.

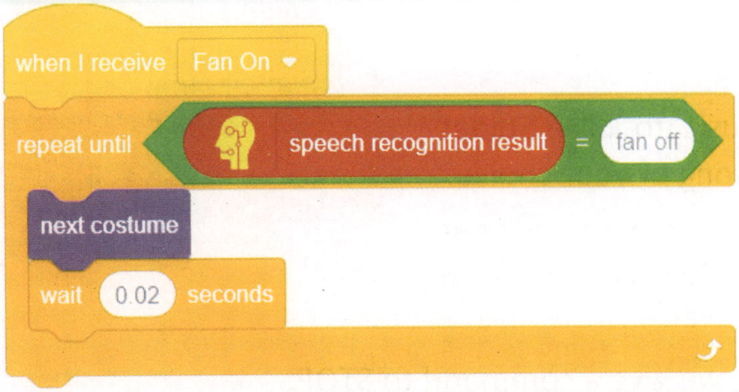

2. Place a when I receive broadcast block and choose Fan ON from the drop-down. We want the fan to rotate till we give it a command to STOP.
3. Place a repeat until block from the Controls palette.
4. Drag and drop an equal to block inside it.
5. Place speech recognition result in first input and write fan off in the second.
6. To make the fan look like it is rotating, we make switch its costumes one after another.
7. Place a next costume block from Looks palette and add a wait of 0.02 seconds.

Turning the Fan OFF

Now write script to stop the fan.

1. Duplicate the above block and choose Fan Off from the drop-down and remove all the blocks.
2. Place a switch costume block below the hat block to stop the rotation of the fan.
3. With this, the script to control the fan is complete.

Script for the Music

Now write the script to turn the Music ON and OFF.

1. Go to the Music sprite.
2. Initialize the looks and the position of the fan sprite as soon as the green flag is clicked.
3. Place a when flag clicked hat block.
4. From the Looks palette, using the set size to block, set its size to 65%.
5. Switch the costume to Music-1.
6. Set the initial position use go to x () y () block from the Motion palette and write 100 in x and -45 in the y.

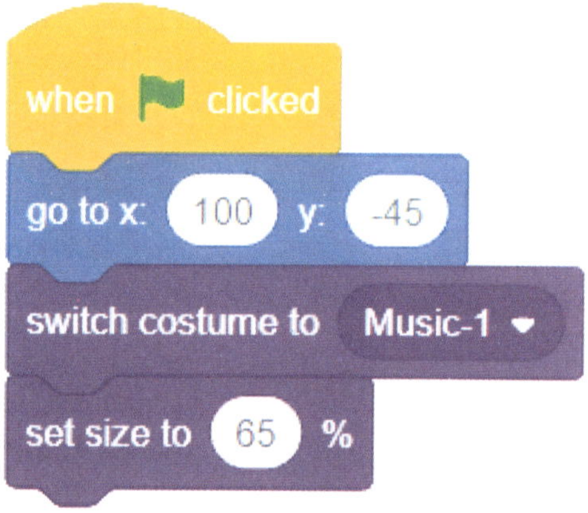

Turning the Music ON

1. We want the Music to play Spider man song or the song of your choice.
2. Place a when I receive broadcast hat block and choose "Music On" from the drop-down.
3. To stop the music, we give a command to STOP.
4. Place a repeat until block from the Controls palette.
5. Drag and drop an equal to block inside it.
6. Place speech recognition result in first input and write "Music Off" in the second.
7. To add the Human Beatbox sound, go to the Sound tab. From the Sound library, choose the Human Beatbox1.
8. From the Sound palette drag and drop the play sound until done and place Human Beatbox1.

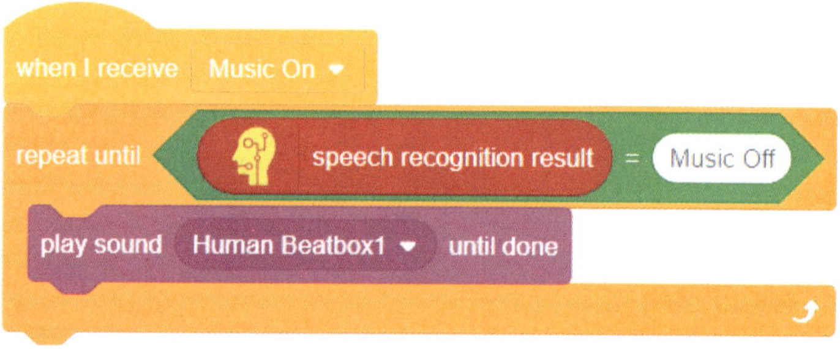

9. Now change the costume of the Music to make it look like it is playing.
10. Make duplicate of this block and remove the play sound block.
11. Place next costume block from the Looks palette and to make it look like it is changing, place the wait block of 0.2 seconds.

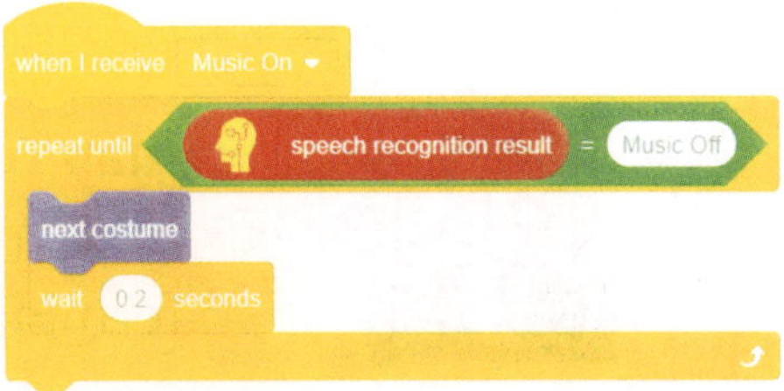

Turning the Music OFF

1. To make the Music stop, duplicate this block and choose Music ON from the drop-down.
2. Remove all the blocks from and place the switch costume to block from the Looks palette and choose Music-1 from the drop-down.

   Your script is ready.

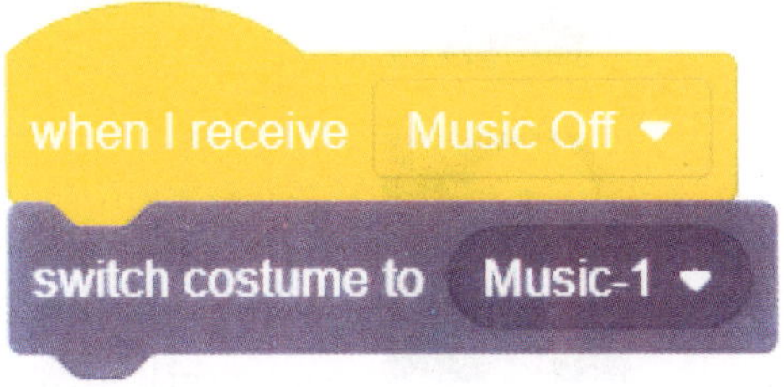

Additional Script for AC

In the above code of blocks, we have not placed the blocks for AC. You can also add these blocks as done for Fan or Lights.

Script for the AC

Let us make the AC run.

1. Go to the AC sprite.
2. Initialize the looks and the position of the AC sprite as soon as the green flag is clicked.
3. Place a when flag clicked hat block.
4. From the Looks palette, using the set size to block, set its size to 70%.
5. Switch the costume to AC.
6. To set the initial position use go to x () y () block from the Motion palette and write 166 in x and 69 in the y.

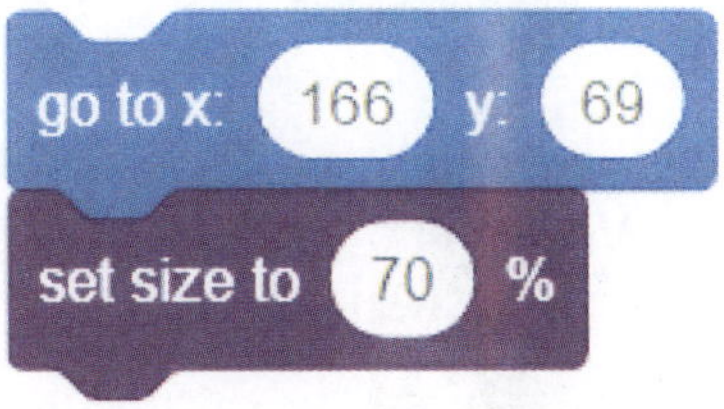

Turning the AC ON

To turn AC ON as soon as we command AC ON.

1. Place a when I receive broadcast block and choose AC ON from the drop-down.
2. For keeping the AC ON until we give command it to STOP, place a repeat until block from the Controls palette.
3. Drag and drop an equal to block inside it.
4. Place speech recognition result in first input and write AC Off in the second.

SCIENTISTS AND THEIR INVENTIONS IN THE FIELD OF ARTIFICIAL INTELLIGENCE	
	**Alan Turing (1912-1954)** Alan Turing detailed a procedure in 1950, known as the Turing Test, forming the basis for Artificial Intelligence.
	**Allen Newell (1927-1992)** Allen Newel was an American Computer Scientist. He developed the first true Artificial Intelligence program, the Logic Theorist, in 1955.
	**Arthur Samuel (1901 - 1990)** He coined the term "machine learning" and created the Samuel Checkers-Playing program. It was one of the world's first successful self-learning programs in 1957.
	**Ross Quillian (1943)** Ross Quillian was a leading scientist and researcher in 1960's. His project Synthex is a contribution to Artificial Intelligence.
	**Edward Feigenbaum (1936)** He created EPAM, one of the first computer models of human learning for his thesis project. The Dendral project used computer systems to identify and communicate the presence of diseases when given spectrometer readings of blood samples.
	**Marvin Minsky (1927 – 2016)** Minsky coined the term perceptron in his groundbreaking work concerning artificial neural networks. Minsky also created models for AI systems.
	**John McCarthy (1927 – 2011)** He was an American mathematician and computer scientist who was a pioneer in the field of artificial intelligence (AI). His main research in the field involved the formalization of commonsense knowledge.
	**Geoffrey Hinton (1947)** He has been one of the researchers who introduced the backpropagation algorithm and the first to use backpropagation for learning word embeddings. He designs machine learning algorithms. His research areas are in deep learning, speech recognition and object classification.

FACT FILE

Turing Test

Alan Mathison Turing
(1912 - 1954)
Mathematician and
Computer Scientist

In 1950, Alan Turing, a great Mathematician introduced a test to check whether a machine can think like a human or not.

In his test, Turing proposed that a computer can be said to be an intelligent if it can mimic human response under specific conditions.

The Turing test is a totally random conversation with no pre-determined topics or questions, meaning that the computer would not necessarily be prepared for what will be asked. Conversations with the computers are spontaneous and carried out by normal people.

The Turing test is based on a party game called "Imitation Game," with some modifications. This game involves three players:

Player A – Man

Player B – Woman

Player C – Human Interrogator

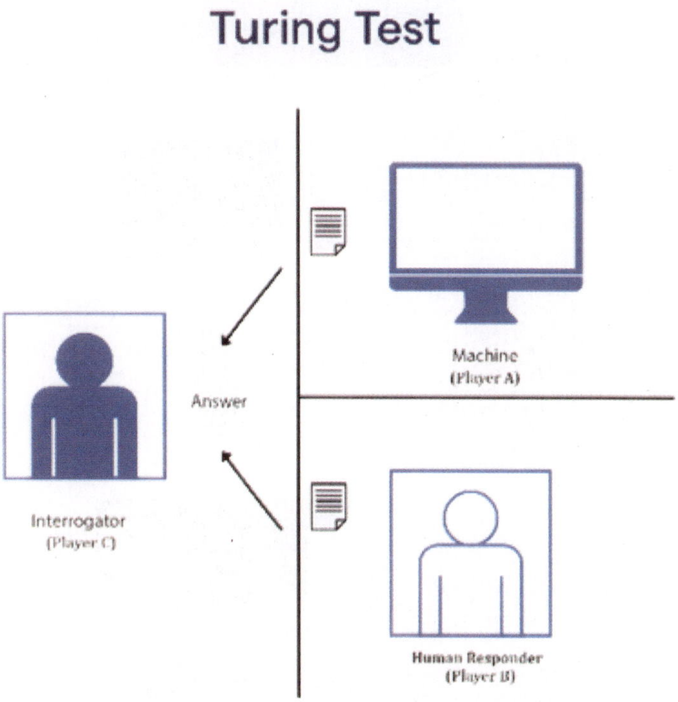

The concept of the game is that the interrogator sits in a room that is separate from both the man (A) and the woman (B).

The goal for the interrogator is to identify who the man is and who the woman is.

Suppose the goal of the man (A) is to deceive the interrogator, meanwhile the woman (B) can attempt to help the interrogator (C). To make this thing fair and unbiased, no verbal cues can be used. Only typewritten questions and answers are sent back and forth.

How does the interrogator know whom to trust?

The interrogator only knows them by X and Y labels and at the end of the game he simply states either 'X is A and Y is B' or 'X is B and Y is A'.

If we remove the man (A) or the woman (B) and replace that person with an intelligent machine, can the machine use its AI system to trick the interrogator (C) into believing that it is a man or a woman?

After modification of the game, the following elements of the game are supposed:

Player A – Computer

Player B – Second Player (A human responder)

Player C – Third Player (A human Interrogator. He is isolated from the other two players and his job is to find that which player is machine among two of them).

The conversation between the players is through the keyboard and screen so that the result should not depend on the machine's ability to convert words as speech.

The test result does not depend on each of the correct answers. It depends on how closely it responses like a human. The computer is permitted to do each and everything possible to force a wrong identification by the interrogator.

VIRTUAL DIGITAL ASSISTANTS

Google Assistant by Google	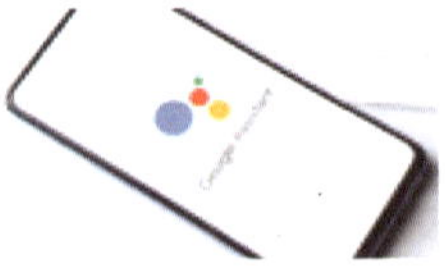
Cortona by Microsoft	
Mycroft by Mycroft AI team	
Siri by Apple	
Amazon Echo by Amazon	

Bixby by Samsung	
Lucida by Samsung	
Cubic by Cubic Robotics	
BlackBerry Assistant by BlackBerry	
Maluuba by Maluuba	

IMMERSIVE TECHNOLOGIES
(Augmented Reality, Virtual Reality)

Augmented Reality

Augmented reality is an enhanced and interactive version of the real-world environment achieved through digital visual elements, sounds and other sensors.

AR consists of three features:

- a combination of digital and real world
- interactions made in real time
- accurate 3D identification of virtual and real-world objects.

The device captures the environment using cameras and sensors.

Data is collected and processed to decide the location of placing the AR objects.

User can view AR object in real-time on the screen.

WORKING OF AUGMENTED REALITY

Virtual Reality

Virtual Reality (VR) is a computer-generated environment with scenes and objects that appear to be real to the users. The users feel that they are immersed in their surroundings.

This VR environment is felt through a device known as a Virtual Reality headset or helmet. VR allows us to immerse ourselves in video games as if we were one of the characters or learn how to perform a surgery or improve the quality of sports training to maximise performance.

Virtual reality removes people from the real world and fully immerses them in a virtual world using a head-mounted display (HMD) or headset. In that virtual world of imagination and sounds, users can move around in all directions, manipulate objects and do many more things. VR is often used in healthcare, architecture and education.

Virtual reality immerses the user in a virtual world through the use of a headset with a screen displaying a virtual environment. The user needs to put a VR headset screen in front of his/her eyes and eliminates any interaction with the real world.

The headset uses head tracking technology, which allows you to look around the environment by physically moving your head. The display will follow whichever direction the user moves, giving him an all-over 360-degree view of the virtual environment.

Goggles and speakers are also used to simulate a real-world experience. In VR, a user can also employ visual, auditory and haptic (touch) stimulation to be immersive in constructed reality.

CHECK YOUR SKILLS IN ARTIFICIAL INTELLIGENCE

1. Which of the following is an example of a Computer Vision program?
   (a) Self-Driving cars
   (b) Face lock in Smartphones
   (c) Both (a) and (b)
   (d) None of these
2. Unscramble the letters and find the correct word to fill in the blank; DATA + ____________ = AI MACHINE
   (a) SMEGSEA
   (b) IMLHOMRGAT
   (c) RROER
   (d) TSMMCOE
3. Unscramble the letters and find the parameter that is *not* used in evaluation stage.
   (a) CMVETEEHAIN
   (b) ONSIPRICE
   (c) RYAUACCC
   (d) ECLARL
4. Which of the following forms of AI is the most advanced?
   (a) Machine Learning
   (b) Deep Learning
   (c) Neural Network
   (d) None of these
5. The Indian Government recently banned a few Apps stating – "Servers in the hostile nation are receiving and using the acquired data improperly". Which terminology suits best for this action?
   (a) AI Ethics
   (b) Data Privacy
   (c) AI Bias
   (d) AI Access
6. Which of the following is the type of data used by NLP applications?
   (a) Images
   (b) Numerical data
   (c) Graphical data
   (d) Text and Speech
7. The 4Ws problem canvas is a part of ____________.
   (a) Problem scoping
   (b) Data acquisition
   (c) Modelling
   (d) Evaluation
8. Choose the five stages of AI project cycle in correct order.
   (a) Evaluation → Problem Scoping → Data Exploration → Data Acquisition → Modelling
   (b) Problem Scoping → Data Exploration → Data Acquisition → Evaluation → Modelling

(c) Data Acquisition → Problem Scoping → Data Exploration → Modelling → Evaluation [ ]

(d) Problem Scoping → Data Acquisition → Data Exploration → Modelling → Evaluation [ ]

9. ____________ helps us to summarise all the key points into one single outline so that in future, whenever there is need to look back at the basis of the problem, we can take a look at it and understand the key elements of it.

(a) 4W Problem canvas [ ] (b) Problem Statement Template [ ]

(c) Data Acquisition [ ] (d) Algorithm [ ]

10. What do you mean by syntax of a language?

(a) Meaning of a sentence [ ] (b) Grammatical structure of a sentence [ ]

(c) Semantics of a sentence [ ] (d) Synonym of a sentence [ ]

11. Read the examples given below:

i. Using Chat GPT to write an email

ii. Face-unlock technology of mobile phones using camera

iii. Turning off lights with IoT device

iv. Hand sanitizer dispenser having sensor

Choose the options that are not the examples of AI.

(a) i and ii [ ] (b) iii and i [ ]

(c) iii and iv [ ] (d) i, iii and iv [ ]

12. An AI system uses two broad classes of data, namely; (i) content data which includes the raw video streams title, description, etc. and (ii) user activity data that includes rating a video, favouriting/liking a video or subscribing to an uploader and watch time.

Based on this, the AI system measures a user's engagement and happiness. It then starts computing personalized recommendations to the user. Which of the following applications can you relate to this?

(a) self-driving car [ ] (b) Siri [ ]

(c) email filters [ ] (d) YouTube [ ]

13. Amazon had been working on a secret AI recruiting tool. The machine-learning specialists uncovered a big problem: their new recruiting engine did not like women. The system taught itself that male candidates were preferable. It penalized resumes that included the word "women". This led to the failure of the tool. This is an example of ____________.

(a) Data Privacy [ ] (b) AI access [ ]

(c) AI Bias [ ] (d) Data Exploration [ ]

14. Srishti learnt about AI terminologies but was not able to recollect the term that is used to refer to machines that perform tasks with vast amounts of data using neural networks. Help her with the correct term.

(a) Fuzzy logic [ ] (b) Deep learning [ ]

(c) Neural learning [ ] (d) Sensing [ ]

15. Rajat has made a model which predicts the performance of Indian Cricket players in upcoming matches. He collected the data of players' performance with respect to stadium, bowlers, opponent team and health. His model works with good accuracy and precision value. Which of the statement given below is incorrect?

(a) Data gathered with respect to stadium, bowlers, opponent team and health is known as Testing Data. [ ]

(b) Data given to an AI model to check accuracy and precision is Testing Data. [ ]

(c) Training data and testing data are acquired in the Data Acquisition stage. [ ]

(d) Training data is always larger as compared to testing data. [ ]

16. Aditi developed a chatbot that clarifies the doubts of science students. She trained the software with lots of data sets catering to all difficulty levels. If any student would type or ask questions related to science, the software would give an instant reply. Identify the domain of AI in the given scenario.

(a) Computer Vision [ ] (b) Data Science [ ]

(c) Natural Language Processing [ ] (d) None of these [ ]

17. This question consists of two statements, namely Assertion (A) and Reason (R). For selecting the correct answer, you have to carefully read the options and select the correct answer.

Assertion (A): The elif is short for else if and is useful to avoid excessive indentation.

Reason (R): The elif statement is placed between the if statement and the else statement.

(a) Both assertion (A) and reason (R) are true and reason (R) is correct explanation of assertion (A). [ ]

(b) Both assertion (A) and reason (R) are true and reason (R) is not correct explanation of assertion (A). [ ]

(c) Assertion (A) is true but reason (R) is false. [ ]

(d) Both assertion (A) and reason (R) are false. [ ]

CASE STUDY

Read the following case study and answer the questions given below:

Turing machine is a fundamental concept in the theory of computation and plays an important role in the field of Computer Science. This machine was first described by the mathematician and Computer Scientist Alan Turing in 1936 and provides a mathematical model of a simple abstract computer.

In the context of theory of computation, Turing machine is used to study the properties of algorithms and to determine what problems can and cannot be solved by computers. They provide a way to model the behaviour of algorithms and to analyse their computational complexity, which is the limit of time and memory they require to solve a problem.

1. Which of the following is true with regard to Turing machine?
   (a) A Turing machine is a computer
   (b) A Turing machine is a combination of computers
   (c) Turing machine contains several physical devices
   (d) The main role of a Turing machine is as a tool to reason about the limits of computation
2. Turing machine is still used today in ______________.
   (a) Computer Science as a research and teaching tool
   (b) Machine learning
   (c) Deep learning
   (d) Natural language processing
3. Turing machine can be used to analyse ______________.
   (a) whether a problem is solvable by a computer
   (b) general knowledge questions
   (c) artificial intelligence of the systems
   (d) machine learning strength of a system

Answer Sheet

CHAPTER-1

Write T for True or F for False : 1. F, 2. T, 3. T, 4. T, 5. F, 6. F, 7. T, 8. F, 9. F, 10. F, 11. T, 12. F

Tick ✓ the best alternatives : 1. (b), 2. (b), 3. (c), 4. (c), 5. (d), 6. (a), 7. (c), 8. (d), 9. (d), 10. (a), 11. (c), 12. (d), 13. (c), 14. (d), 15. (b), 16. (c), 17. (b), 18. (c), 19. (a), 20. (a)

Competency Based Questions : 1. (a), 2. The technique is named as OCR and it uses natural language processing., 3. (a) Future me: (1) computer games, (2) game player, (3) Mario, Contra, Pac-Man, (4) taking over the world, (5) playing games with joystick, (6) play with mouse, (7) parrot, (8) dog, (9) graduate to apply for the jobs (10) black and white monitor, (11) to know that you are writing computer programs, (12) for reminding the old TV and computer games, (b) past you

CHAPTER-2

Write T for True or F for False : 1. T, 2. T, 3. T, 4. T, 5. F

Tick ✓ the best alternatives : 1. (b), 2. (c), 3. (d), 4. (d), 5. (d), 6. (d), 7. (c), 8. (d), 9. (d), 10. (c)

CHAPTER-3

Write T for True or F for False : 1. F, 2. F, 3. F, 4. T , 5. T

Tick ✓ the best alternatives : 1. (d), 2. (a), 3. (b), 4. (b), 5. (d), 6. (c), 7. (b), 8. (d), 9. (c)

Competency Based Questions : 1. Sustainable management of water and sanitation (SDG 6), 2.Responsible Consumption and Production (SDG 12), 3. End Poverty (SDG 1), 4. Growth and Employment (SDG 8), 5. Gender Equality (SDG 5), 6. Combat Climate Change (SDG 13), 7. Peaceful and Inclusive Societies (SDG 16), 8. End Hunger (SDG 2), 9. Life on Land (SDG 15), 10. Partnerships for the Goals (SDG 17), 11. Healthy Life (SDG 3), 12. Life below water (SDG 14), 13. Safe Human Settlements and Cities (SDG 11), 14. Reduce Inequality among countries (SDG 10), 15. Inclusive and Quality Education (SDG 4), 16. Sustainable and Modern Energy (SDG 7), 17. Sustainable Infrastructure (SDG 9)

CHAPTER-4

Write T for True or F for False : 1. F, 2. T, 3. F, 4. T, 5. F, 6. T, 7. T

Tick ✓ the best alternatives : 1. (d), 2. (c), 3. (a), 4. (c), 5. (b)

CHAPTER-5

Write T for True or F for False : 1. F, 2. T, 3. T, 4. T, 5. F

Tick ✓ the best alternatives : 1. (b), 2. (d), 3. (c), 4. (c)

Competency Based Question : 1. (d)

CHAPTER-6

Write T for True or F for False : 1. T, 2. F, 3. F, 4. F, 5. T

Tick ✓ the best alternatives : 1. (a), 2. (a), 3. (b), 4. (c), 5. (c), 6. (b), 7. (b), 8. (c), 9. (d), 10. (d), 11. (b), 12. (b), 13. (d), 14. (b), 15. (c), 16. (c), 17. (c), 18. (c), 19. (a)

QUIZ TIME

1. (c), 2. Words are: MESSAGE, ALGORITHM, ERROR, COMMENTS and correct answer is (b) ALGORITHM, 3. Words are: ACHIEVEMENT, PRECISION, ACCURACY, RECALL and correct answer is (a), 4. (b), 5. (b), 6. (d), 7. (a), 8. (d), 9. (b), 10. (b), 11. (c), 12. (d), 13. (c), 14. (b), 15. (a), 16. (c), 17. (b)

Case Study : 1. (d), 2. (a), 3. (a)